TALES OF THE
RESISTANCE

TALES OF THE
RESISTANCE

D A V I D   A N D   K A R E N   M A I N S

Chariot Books
DAVID C.COOK PUBLISHING CO.

Illustrated by Jack Stockman

Chariot Books is an imprint of David C. Cook Publishing Co.
David C. Cook Publishing Co., Elgin, Illinois 60120
David C. Cook Publishing Co., Weston, Ontario

TALES OF THE RESISTANCE

First printing, 1986
Printed in the United States of America
90 89 88 87 86   1 2 3 4 5

Library of Congress Cataloging-in-Publication Data
Mains, David R.
    Tales of the resistance.
    Sequel to: Tales of the kingdom.
    Summary. Twelve incidents in the Resistance against the Enchanter, in which residents of the Enchanted City are rescued by the King or his followers as they strive for the Restoration of the Kingdom.
    [1. Fantasy] I. Mains, Karen Burton. II. Stockman, Jack, 1951-   ill.
III. Title.
PZ7.M2782Tar   [Fic]   86-2319
ISBN 0-89191-938-4

To His Majesty,
my Sovereign Liege;
to His Eminence,
the Benevolent Potentate;
to His Supreme Holiness,
the Lord Monseigneur;
to His Most Royal Highness,
the Monarch of All—
to the King!
and to the Restoration of His Kingdom!

Table of Contents

Back to Enchanted City

Once upon a time there was a lad, with boyhood behind him and manhood close, who heard the call of the King to follow him into Enchanted City and do the work of the Kingdom. . . .

Hero was afraid.

He watched the Ranger hold a burning torch to the ring of stones that circled the place of the Great Celebration. The Sacred Flames ignited with a w-o-o-O-O-O-SH, lifting the hems of the blue robes of the protectors of Great Park, who stood as sentries around Inmost Circle. The silver insignia of the Rangers caught the light and flashed in the outer circle around the rim of fire.

Tonight he would leave these friends, leave Mercie and Caretaker, leave these woods, these dear fields, leave everything in the world he had come to love. *Well, almost everything,* he reminded himself: What he loved most in the world was the King and to be a King's man and to do the King's work.

And the voice of that King, the most beautiful of men, had spoken inwardly only this morning: *It is time. It is time to begin the restoration of the Kingdom. I need a King's man with a hero's heart. Will you come?*

Far off, Ranger horns sounded from the watchtowers that guarded Deepest Forest. *Croi-croi!* Come-come! *Croi-Croi!* Come to Inmost Circle! Come to the solemn assembly!

Hero watched as the people he loved made entrance, passed through the Sacred Flames and became real. He watched Amanda step into the fire a ragtag tomboy and step out a beautiful, graceful princess. He watched the unhappy woman who had been the orphan keeper's assistant become someone with a mother's smile for all the children, who ran to hug her. He saw Caretaker become Ranger Commander.

How can I ever go? thought Hero. *How can I leave all this?* But he had heard the voice of his King: *Come, Hero. It is time.* And he knew he must go.

So this solemn assembly had been hurriedly gathered for the Rite of Adoption, for no lad could go back into Enchanted City an orphan. Orphans belonged to the evil Enchanter. Hero must be someone's son; he must have proof of parentage to protect him.

Dread filled his soul. He thought of the darkness of Enchanted City, where the citizens worked by night and slept by day. He remembered Burning Place where the dead were burned: all who had died of weariness, of hunger, of heartsickness.

In his memory, he saw fire burning the pyre that held his mother's body. (She had always said, "There is a King. A real King!") Death drums began to beat in his mind: *oo-mb-pha . . . oo-mb-pha . . . oo-mb-pha-din.* Visions of Burners with hot brands and smoldering pokers flashed. He heard the blows of the Breakers. The song of the Naysayers, *nay-nay-nay, nay-nay-nay, nay-nay-nay,* clutched his heart with icy fingers.

He remembered Branding—himself a screaming five-year-old—and how the hot iron had seared his cheek. For the first time in many months, Hero touched the scar. Here, in this place among these people, he was Hero, loved by many. In that terrible place, he was nothing but scum. The people of Enchanted City would point and jeer in the old way—Scarboy! Scarboy!

S-C-A-R-B-O-Y!!

Suddenly, Hero heard a scream rise out of Enchanted City and fall with a paralyzing moan in his own soul. He raised up his head, startled. It was more than memory. Hero knew it was the voice of the evil Enchanter from the dark midst of the Dagoda, with his fiery head thrown back, with fire priests dancing and their ceremonial bells jangling: *jchang-jchang-jchang.*

S-C-A-R-B-O-Y!!

Hero cowered, standing outside the Circle of Flames. His heart felt like stone. The hot eye of the Enchanter had found him, here in his fear. How could he follow the King if he kept hearing this loud and terrible cry? He would be vulnerable, alone.

"Oh, Mercie," the lad whispered to the old, old woman beside him. "I'm afraid. How will I ever find the King? You know I'm not good at recognizing disguises. I can *feel* the Enchanter's hot eye, and hear the *nay-din-nay-din* of Enchanted City, and remember the brands and the blows and the stink of Burning Place."

The old woman took his hand, and Hero felt the strength of her grasp. Mercie smiled. "Hero, fear is ever the Enchanter's ally. Have you forgotten your own powerful weapons?"

Hero gulped and shook his head no—the King's name, the humming hatchet, the music of Great Celebration. No, he had not forgotten. But he doubted; doubted their power in Enchanted City.

Mercie turned, placing both hands on his shoulders. Hero embraced her. When he fled Enchanted City, he had been a child and Mercie had been as tall as he. Now her white head rested on his chest, and she felt fragile in his arms.

Her voice, however, was heart high.

"Walk right through the fear, Hero. Speak any of the names—His Majesty, His Royal Highness, the One Lord King—and you will outstare any tormentor who faces you. Learn the hum of the hatchet, and no *nay-din-nay*, no *oo-mb-pha* will frighten you. Sing the music of the Great Celebration; dance the steps, and you will kick aside the ashes of death."

With that, the two, still holding hands, passed through the Circle of Sacred Flames and became real: Mercie, young and beautiful, and he—with a shock, Hero realized he was now wearing the blue cloak of a Ranger.

Tonight there was no glad clamor of welcome. Instead, the subjects of the King parted in solemn silence as Hero and Mercie walked slowly to the center of Inmost Circle. The quiet was filled with portent. Everyone knew he was returning to Enchanted City.

Ranger Commander stood tall and strong in the middle and raised his hand in salute as the two approached. At this signal, the blue-cloaked men and women acting as sentries passed inward through the flames.

"Ranger initiate!" called out Commander. "Stand forth for Revealing!"

With a pounding heart, Hero obeyed. He had always longed to be a Ranger, a protector of Great Park, but never, never had he felt so unworthy as at this moment.

Kneeling and bowing, Hero felt Ranger Commander's hand placed firmly on his head. The voice which always filled him with awe spoke above him.

"Tonight we are gathered to induct the lad Hero into the corps of Rangers, protectors and watchkeepers for the King. What is your pleasure?"

The blue-cloaked men and women spoke as one: "Let the ceremony begin!"

The awful first question was asked: "Does anyone know just cause why this one, Hero, should not be invested with the office of Ranger?"

Each Ranger in the circle answered in turn.

"I do not," said the first.

"Nor do I," called out the next.

The lad kneeled in an agony of suspense. He longed with all his being for this office, but he wished someone would speak to his unworthiness before he shamed them all by being a faithless Ranger.

"Nor I—nor I." And so, round the circle came the pledges of faith. Hero could hardly believe that not one Ranger would show just cause that he was unworthy.

Then the second awful question: "Do you, initiate, hold just cause against yourself?"

Hero sighed deeply. Revealing demanded honesty. Lifting his head, he looked into Commander's eyes, "Sire, I—I am afraid. I am afraid of the task at hand."

A murmur went up from the blue-cloaked circle. A voice cried, "No just cause! Even the most courageous fear the unknown task!"

Hero gulped. "But Sire, I—I doubt. The mettle of the powers is unknown to me. I fear its weakness against the force of Enchanted City."

Another voice cried, "Power is always untested until it has been tried. No just cause!"

Hero spoke one last time. "Sire, my seeing is dim, and the voice of the Enchanter is near."

Ranger Commander answered, "Dim sight is cured by choosing to see. We hear the voice of whomever we allow near. No just cause. Stand forth!"

Hero rose from his knees. Ranger Commander called above his head, "What is the pleasure of this company? Shall we induct this Hero, once of Enchanted City, now of Great Park, for the task at hand?"

A hurrah went up from the circle of Rangers, followed by another larger shout from the crowd standing beyond. "To vows! To vows!"

Hero's heart swelled with this honor. He would be a Ranger. He would fight for the King. He would give his forever pledge to protect the Kingdom, to be faithful. "To the King!" he shouted.

"To the King!" all shouted back.

"To the Restoration!"

With that, Commander turned to Hero and offered his hand. "Welcome, Ranger. The world goes not well, but the Kingdom comes." For the first time, the lad's hand was taken in the Ranger clasp where each held the wrist of the other. Hero noticed the strong pulse beneath his fingers, and he felt joined to the life of the other.

"Now," said Mercie beside him, "the Rites of Adoption." The beautiful woman pressed two fingers to Hero's forehead. She steadied the back of his head with her other hand. The Rangers in the near circle lifted their hatchets, blades pointed toward him, and a hum, one note only, began.

"I, wife of Caretaker, war-maiden Ranger, do implant you, Ranger Hero, with this proof of parentage. You will always know you belong to us. You are ours. Orphan no more, you are heir to all we hold."

Hero closed his eyes and listened to the simple one-note hum. The place on his forehead which Mercie touched grew warm; then the gentle warmth diffused through his whole body. It was only when he opened his eyes that he realized every hatchet had been sheathed and that the hum he heard, the one-note hum, was now in his own brain, in his own ears, in is own heart.

The people of Great Park began to leave; wordlessly, they withdrew into Deepest Forest. Amanda gave him a shy hug. Her eyes glistened with tears. On the edge of the crowd, special friends waved silent farewells. Each Ranger clasped his hand and then departed. The Sacred Flames dimmed and died, leaving only glowing charcoals to mark the circle.

Hero stood alone with Caretaker and old Mercie.

"It is time," said Caretaker. "We will accompany you as far as Burning Place."

So the three walked together out of Inmost Circle, through Deepest Forest, past the practice field, deserted in the night, along the path by Caretaker's cottage where the latest outcasts rested in sleep, down the edge of Wildflower Woods to the old stone gates of Great Park.

A faint melon-wedge of light cracked the night sky, and Hero realized he would leave Great Park at the same time of day, dawn, that he had once entered it so many seasons ago.

Caretaker raised his hatchet and the familiar hymn-hum began. The gates creaked open slowly, and the three walked beneath the inscription: WELCOME ALL WHO HUNT.

Hero turned and watched the gates close behind him. "Will I ever see this place again?" he wondered out loud.

Mercie pulled him around to face Enchanted City. "Nonsense," she snapped. "You'll see it every time you close your eyes." Little as she was, she was now without pity and her grasp was mighty on his arm.

The two old people walked on either side of the boy. Hero dragged his heavy feet through the garbage dump, filled with rotten refuse, which separated Great Park from Enchanted City. Closer they came, closer and closer to Burning Place, just outside the city walls. And all the while, Hero sensed that Mercie and Caretaker were growing fainter, dimming somehow here in the rank air that smelled of smoke and fire. They were fading away from him. In the soft light, Hero read a sign which proclaimed:

THERE IS NO SUCH THING AS A KING.
DEATH TO PRETENDERS!

His feet kicked the soft ashes, and Hero knew he had finally returned, come back to the one place that he hated above all others.

"Mercie," he whispered. "Caretaker?"

They were gone.

They had left him here on the edge of Burning Place, alone, without aid. Abandoned. Helpless. Unloved. No, no wait. Hero took a deep breath.

He closed his eyes and thought back to where he had just been. Inmost Circle. Within the leaping Sacred Flames. He remembered the cry, "To vows!" and recalled the strong pulse of life clasped in the Ranger grasp. He was not alone. He might be on the edge of the evil Enchanted City, but wonderful things had happened to him. He belonged to somebody. He was loved.

At that moment, with his eyes still closed, he heard the lovely hum. It was not just a memory out of the past. It was with him now, in his ears, in his own brain. As Hero listened, the flailing in his heart was quieted. The hum grew from one note to many, and from many notes to the full music of Great Celebration.

And there in the light of dawn, of a new day, as the people of the city ended their work and prepared to sleep, Hero lifted his head and held forth his arms. His back straightened, Ranger tall, and he began the dance, kicking the ashes of Burning Place as he stepped to the glorious chords of the inward melody. And for those who were still awake to hear, a laugh, young and joyous, rose from outside the walls and settled in the morning air.

For the lad, Hero, discovered that when one belongs to the Kingdom, he is never alone in the terrible places of the world; he can always hear the single, clear-note hum.

Doubletalk, Triple Tongue, And Theysay

*Heralds stood on broadcast columns throughout
Enchanted City and shouted news. They announced special events
as well as the hour of the night. Because of power-outs,
however, no one rally knew the correct time. One herald might
proclaim, "Midnight. All's well!" while another shouted
"Ten-thirty o'clock. Half-night approaches!" No wonder citizens
suffered from indigestion, they were always eating dinner
at the wrong hour.*

Doubletalk, Triple Tongue, and Theysay were friends. The three boys had grown up in Moire Oxan, the tenement slums which stretched for miles, hovel stacked upon hovel. Together they endured illness, poverty, hunger, and branding. When Theysay's parents died, the other two helped him escape orphan dragnets by hiding him back and forth in their own tenement hovels, at great risk of penalty to themselves.

All were now heralds of the Enchanter—and proud of their accomplishment. It was something for penniless young men to rise to heraldship, to stand on the tall broadcast columns, trusted with all the news fit to proclaim. It was something for ragtag ruffians to wear the red and yellow jerseys with the Enchanter's insignia of blazing fire. It was something to blow the herald horn whenever the wizard's sleek black limousine moved ominously through the city streets, and to shout, "The Enchanter is coming! Make way for the Enchanter!"

Unfortunately, heralds frequently made contradictory announcements. One might shout, "Melons in the marketplace! First come, first served!" while the herald on the very next post was shouting, "No melons today! Try rutabagas in your fruit salad!"

Some people suspected that heralds were chosen only if they had something wrong with their speech. Some heralds spoke backwards, "!gnimoc si retnahcnE ehT" Some had twisted tongues. Some had lockmouth, so that all s's whistled through clenched teeth with a wicked his-s-s-s-s-s. Some had very bad breath.

Doubletalk made positive announcements out of one side of his mouth. "The Enchanter is coming!", for instance, or, "Melons in the marketplace!" would be announced out of the right side. Negative announcements, however, would be shouted out of the left side of his mouth: "The Enchanter is not coming!" "The melons have all been stolen!"

Trouble began when Doubletalk couldn't decide if the announcement was negative or positive. Was the theft of rutabagas good or bad news? Or, maybe, it was a good thing that the Enchanter *wasn't* coming.

Consequently, he began to make announcements out of both sides of his mouth. "The Enchanter is coming!" (on the right side). "The Enchanter is not coming!" (on the left). Then both at the same time. His tongue worked so hard it eventually split in two.

Doubletalk always worked up a sweat, but no one appreciated his great effort. People standing beneath his column shouted, "Heh, bub! Make up yer mind. Watcha got? Wet-noodle brains?" And they threw rotten tomatoes.

Triple Tongue faltered over each word three times. "Th-th-the En-ch-ch-chan-ter is c-c-coming!" he would cry. His announcements took a very long time. After a while, he discovered that if he rushed his words, his tongue wouldn't triple so much. So he learned to shout, "Thenchtiscomn!"

Unfortunately, no one (except Theysay) could understand him. People standing beneath his post would wrinkle their noses and say, "Eh? Wha? Why doncha learn to talk plain?" Then they would rock his post.

The third friend, Theysay, had learned early never to state an opinion of his own. That was bound to get you into trouble. "They say the Enchanter is coming!" he would proclaim, or "They say the Enchanter is not coming!" He never took the blame for anything he said because he only said what they said; and he said what they said even when he knew he shouldn't say it, because he

only said what he said because other people said it!

People beneath his column would look at each other and whisper in amazement, "Did you hear him say what they said?" He was the only herald of the three who ever won popular approval.

One day Triple Tongue said to Doubletalk and Theysay, "S-s-say, I'm-m-m get-get-getting ti-ti-tired of p-p-peop-p-ple s-s-saying, 'Eh?', and-d-ds 'Wha?' and rocking m-m-my post." Triple Tongue felt that heralding might not be all it was cracked up to be.

Doubletalk answered, "That could be bad or again, it might be good. It's probably both, actually."

"Well," said Theysay, "they said that there are a new batch of heralds being trained. They say some of the old heralds will be put to street sweeping. I don't know if what they say is right or not; all I know is that they say it."

The next day Doubletalk had something to report. "An Enchanter's man stood beneath my broadcast post all night. That could be good if I'm in any danger and need protection" (right tongue section) "or it could be bad if I'm not doing my job well, and they want to put a newer herald in my column" (left tongue section). *Blo-o-oe-e-e!* He blew his lips to relax them. His mouth was tired.

Triple Tongue spoke very fast, "Whdyotnkththtsalabot?"

"Eh?" said Doublespeak. "Why don't you just talk plain? I'm tired of *some* people saying things I can't understand."

Triple Tongue sighed. A small tear trickled down his nose and spotted his jersey. He was tired of never being understood.

"He said," translated Theysay, " 'What do you think that's all about?' "

"Oh," said Doubletalk, "why didn't you say so?" He blew out his tired tongue again. *Blo-o-oe-e-e!*

"They say that there's a stranger in the streets talking about another kingdom, and how foolish it is to live in the night, and that we all should follow him and not obey the Enchanter," said Theysay.

"What?" said both of his friends in amazement.

"*I* didn't say it," the third friend answered, shaking his head and backing away. "*They* said it."

The very next night, Triple Tongue noticed a stranger standing beneath his broadcast column. A soft light surrounded the man. Blowing his herald horn, Triple Tongue made an announcement, very quickly, "Mlnsnmktplc! Mlnsnmktplc!"

Triple Tongue heard a nearby taxi honk its horn. HARNK! HARNK!
"Nyah! Nyah!" shouted the people, rocking his post.

As if he didn't have enough troubles with citizens yelling at him and
with the threat of new heralds, now the City Taxi Company was interfering.
Every herald knew about the cabbies, who had banded together to help the
citizens of Enchanted City discover the true news. What a nuisance. One beep
meant yes; two beeps meant no.

He leaned from his column and peered into the shadows. "H-h-how m-
m-many honks did that h-h-horn honk?"

Triple Tongue could barely see the stranger's smile. "The horn blasted
twice, meaning that the news you proclaimed was untrue. The only melons in
the marketplace are moldy, ready for the garbage dump."

"Oh," said Triple Tongue. He had been afraid of that, but why did he
suddenly feel so ashamed? Was it because he had known there were no good
melons in the marketplace? He let his herald horn dangle by his side. Its
ribbon standard drooped in the dust at the top of his column.

"In my kingdom," said the stranger, "we work very hard to speak what is. That way we can learn to trust each other. Your tongue became tripled at Branding. You were afraid then; you are afraid now. Come follow me, and I will take away your fear. Then you can learn to speak a new way."

Suddenly, all of the fears Triple Tongue had ever known rose within. The fear of the hot iron at Branding. The fear of his parents leaving him. The fear of orphan dragnets. The fear of living with the Orphan Keeper. The fear of not being understood. The fear of being understood too much. No wonder his tongue tripped over itself. Could it be possible never to fear again?

Triple Tongue climbed down from his broadcast column. He propped his herald horn against the base and tore the insignia of fire from his herald's jersey. He'd had enough. No one had ever understood him before, not the way this stranger, in one brief moment, understood him.

"But, m-m-my friends?" he asked.

"Take me to them," said the stranger.

Soon they stood beneath Doubletalk's column. He was blowing his horn. Out of the right side of his mouth he announced, "Make way! The Enchanter is coming! Make way!"

A nearby taxi honked its horn. HARNK! HARNK!—not true!

Doubletalk made bubbles out of his weary mouth. *Blo-o-oe-e-e! That Taxi Company. Bunch of troublemakers.* This time he spoke out of the left side, "The Enchanter is not coming!" Then the right, "He-is!" Then the left again, "He's-not!" Then both sides at once, "Is-not-is! Not-is-not!" The herald wiped the sweat off his face and flapped his jersey to cool off in the night air.

The taxi honked twice again. HARNK! HARNK!

The stranger swung his lithe body halfway up the broadcasting column in order to be seen by the exhausted announcer. "It's hard work speaking out of both sides of your mouth. The subjects in my kingdom say yes when they mean yes and no when they mean no. It's a lot less trouble, believe me."

Doubletalk sighed. Who was this nuisance? Interfering with the official function of heraldy: Code 345. He'd better watch it or the Enchanter's eye would be on him.

"You're tired, Doubletalk," said the stranger. "You need a good rest. You've been working too hard at all the wrong things. Come join me, and I'll teach you to work at what really is."

Doubletalk pulled the sweaty jersey over his head and hung it on a nail on his broadcasting column. It was time for his nightly break anyway. He

admitted to himself that the stranger was right. He was tired of wearing this heraldry attire with its ridiculous stripes (oh, but often he loved it). He was tired of blowing this silly horn (but sometimes he blew it well and it sounded wonderful). He hated for people to call him a noodle brain (but then, perhaps he was). He climbed wearily down from the post and extinguished his night-light as a sign that he was taking ten.

Together, Triple Tongue and Doubletalk and the stranger started out to find Theysay. He was heralding the time: "They say, 'It's half-past five!' They say, 'Daybreak is approaching!' They say, 'It's time to get ready for bed!' "

The stranger stood beneath the column. "Actually, they are wrong. People were made to live in the light. In my kingdom, they work and play during the day and sleep at night."

"Who says?" challenged Theysay, but he wondered how dawn surrounded the stranger. *They* must have been wrong again about daybreak.

The stranger suddenly tossed back his head and laughed. The sound was amazing in this street at night, in this place where little laughter was ever heard. He pointed to himself confidently, "I say! I have always said! I say now and will always say: Live in the light!"

For the first time, Theysay realized how sick he was of what everyone else said. He put a hand on his hip and thought to himself, *Who cares?* The words of the stranger struck him. How wonderful! How bold! How forthright! *I say! I say!*

The herald thought he would try these words himself, "Uh, I say—you're right. That's what I say." Oh, they felt so good, these words on his tongue. His heart leaped within him. He vaulted from the top of the column, swinging round and round down to its base. "I say!" he shouted. "The man's right! Live in the light!" He put his herald horn to his lips and blew.

The stranger drew the three of them into a close huddle, "Listen to me closely. What really matters is that you learn to live by what I say. Come! Be a part of my kingdom and learn a new way!"

From somewhere in the distance, another herald proclaimed, "The Enchanter is coming! Make way!" The friends lifted their heads, fear flashing in their eyes. Nearby, a taxi honked a warning. HARNK! True! The Enchanter really was coming!

Doubletalk began to jiggle on his toes. "Oh, oh, oh, now we're in for it." He shouted as though he had never left his post. "The Enchanter is coming! The Enchanter is coming!"

"How about a ride?" asked the stranger, with a grim smile. He didn't seem to be afraid, but he was in a hurry. He snapped his fingers and the nearby taxi gunned its motor, turned on headlights, accelerated, and then screeched to a stop at the curb beside them. The Stranger opened the back door. "Going my way?" he asked the three.

Herald horns began to blow from post to post, announcing the imminent arrival of the fire wizard. Triple Tongue rushed into the taxi. He leaned forward to look out at his two friends. "Hurry! Hurry! Are you com-m-ming? Doubletalk-k-k! Th-th-theysay?"

Both heralds shook their heads. Doubletalk turned his back and hastened to man his post again. Theysay stood, paralyzed by fear.

"Make way! The Enchanter is coming!" cried a herald. "Make way!"

"Doubletalk!" yelled Triple Tongue. "Come back!"

Theysay took a few steps away from the taxi.

A long, black limousine turned the corner at the end of the street. They could all see its ghostly driver. Doubletalk ran toward it, waving it down and pointing back in their direction.

The cabbie stretched across and jerked the handle to close the back door.

The stranger, still standing on the curb, leaned through the front window. "Tell Big Operator I sent—"

Suddenly Theysay turned back and shouted, "Wait! Wait! Don't go without me! I say I want to come with you!"

The door was opened again, the boy jumped inside, and the taxi sped off. The two friends jostled and bounced against each other as the cab careened wildly through side streets. Disconnected from the powerline, the taxi ran mysteriously on its own, hiding in dark unlit alleys and then cruising into a dark garage where a great overhead door slammed shut behind them.

"Wh-who should we say sent us?" whispered Triple Tongue.

"Yes," said Theysay. "Who was that stranger?"

"Doncha know?" asked the cabbie. "Why, that guy's the King!"

So the two boys joined the resistance of the King and worked for the restoration of the Kingdom—one without fear and the other with new confidence. They loved the new language they learned to speak, the language of the subjects of the Kingdom, the King's very own words. And they remembered with sorrow their friend Doubletalk, who was soon appointed to the post of Chief Herald to the Enchanter.

The Taxi Resistance

Some people in Enchanted City said that taxis could get you wherever you needed to go, even in power outs. Some people said that the City Taxi Company was not afraid of Burners and Breakers and Naysayers—but no one said it very loudly.

The sharp wind moaned through the flop hole where Hero tried to sleep. These lonely weeks in Enchanted City had been dreadful. He was hungry and cold and felt lost. Above all, though he was ashamed to admit it, he was afraid.

No one would give him work, and what little money he had was running low. He had no idea how to sight the King, and the ominous spell of the Enchanter was weighing his heart with leaden dread. Hero longed for the daylight of Great Park, for Caretaker and Mercie, for the laughter of friends, for the comforting sound of the watchkeepers crying, "But the Kingdom comes!" He longed for home.

Light spilled through the cracks in the rickety shelters of Moire Oxan. The sentry cry of patrols disturbed the slumber of the weary people. *Sleep in the light!*

Sleep in the light! they warned. Hero couldn't sleep.

Hero feared the wandering patrols. He knew an ugly scar on his cheek was evidence of branding, but he wasn't sure this Enchanter's mark would satisfy interrogators. Wouldn't a Breaker demand proof of identity? Some surer certificate of adoption than the note humming in his heart?

Hero despaired. Where was the King? How was he to be found? And what part was Hero supposed to play in the Restoration?

Nay-nay-nay, nay-nay-nay sounded the dread melody of the Naysayers. *Nothing can be done; nothing will be done.* Hero tried to hum a tune from the dance of the Great Celebration, but the melody was faint. He kept thinking: I am only a lad after all. The Enchanter is powerful and his league is mighty.

He coughed. The stink of Enchanted City always choked his lungs. Suddenly he heard the dreadful sound that all the people feared. *Oo-mb-pha . . . Oo-mb-pha . . . Oo-mb-pha-din.* The pounding of the death drums. Another dragnet. He had escaped one only yesterday and been forced to find a different flop hole. Hunting orphans, the Enchanter's men conducted sweeping day raids in Moire Oxan, waking citizens from their sleep.

Hero could hear the drums and then the Naysayers again, those singers who chanted tunes that smothered hope. He could hear the boot tromp of the Burners and Breakers, the Enchanter's secret police, running up and down flimsy fire exits. Suddenly, cudgels were hammering on doors in his very building. He heard children crying. *They have come for me,* he thought. *What can I do? Where can I hide?*

WHAM! The door to his flop hole banged open. Two Burners rushed in, their pokers flaring. A ghastly Breaker grabbed him from his mat.

"Identification!" ordered one of the secret police.

Hero was numb. *What can I say?* He turned to his meager pack of belongings and saw the handle of the hatchet Caretaker had given him.

"One moment," he mumbled. Hero bent to grab the handle and then turned swiftly, swinging the hatchet in front of him. His heart leapt in terror as he waited for a mighty blow to crush his skull. But to his amazement, the lights of the Burners' pokers glowed dimmer. Cautiously, slowly, all three backed toward the broken door.

"To the King! To my Sovereign Liege Lord! To the One Monarch of All!" Hero cried.

Power from the hatchet throbbed in his hand; his heart grew brave at his own shouting of the Names. He lifted his tool and backed the Burners and the

Breakers step by step out of the hole and down the outside fire exit. In the daylight, from the top of the rickety stairs, he could see that a circle of frightened children had been rounded up on the street. All were blindfolded so they would not see the light and thereby remember the look of day.

Hero remembered when he had escaped form Enchanted City, a terrified orphan with death drums and Burners in pursuit. He recalled how he had raced to safety with his little brother in his arms. *If I can save just one more child from the Enchanter, if I can keep one child from a life of bondage, if I can carry one child to Mercie, my return to Enchanted City will have been worth it.*

Standing at the top of the fire exit, Hero raised his hatchet above his head. Anger flooded him, and he let forth a mighty shout, "I am Hero, Ranger of Great Park! A King's man!"

There was a moment of silence. The death drums paused; the chant of the Naysayers ceased. The whole sleeping city seemed to listen to his shout.

Din . . . din . . . din . . . The death drums were sounding another beat, faster and faster—a battle beat. Hero realized that more Burners and Breakers were gathering in striking formation. He had done a foolhardy thing. Even with the hatchet in hand, he was only one against many. He was in the middle of the Enchanter's territory, with no fellow Ranger to come to his aid. His only chance was in taking his opponents by surprise.

Rushing down the stairs, Hero swung into the battle tactic he had learned in the War of Fire in Great Park. "To the King! To the Restoration!" he cried, holding his hatchet with both hands. He jumped into the middle of the band of captured orphans. "Scatter!" he shouted. "Take off your blindfolds and run!"

With his weapon at arm's length, Hero began to whirl as the children scattered, climbing stairs, turning street corners, scurrying into holes. Round and round Hero whirled, cutting a circle of emptiness between himself and his would-be captors.

The Enchanter's men were so intent on taking him prisoner, they let the children escape. For a moment, Hero felt a defiant gladness.

S-C-A-R-B-O-Y! S-C-A-R-B-O-Y!

The Enchanter's evil eye had spotted him. The moment his old name was shouted, Hero began to freeze. His feet were leaden; the hatchet felt so heavy. Closer and closer inched the Burners and Breakers. One of the Breakers caught Hero's eye and held it with a stare; then he lifted his ugly cudgel over his head.

HARNK-HARNK! HARNK-HARNK! From opposite directions two taxicabs came careening down the narrow alley, their horns blaring, their speed frightening. *HARNK-HARNK!*

The Enchanter's men scattered, and the taxis screeched to a stop within inches of the stunned Hero.

"Need a ride, buddy?" A burly arm grabbed Hero and pulled him roughly into the front seat. As Hero frantically yanked the door shut behind him, his cab blasted into reverse and squealed around another corner. Within seconds a whole fleet of taxis raced out of alleys and side streets. They drove for a while in a straight line, and then veered off in opposite directions. *HARNK! HARNK! HARNK!* Their horns blared in great commotion, and for a moment Hero felt safe. No pursuer would know which cab had kidnapped him.

But was he under arrest or under protection?

Hero could just read the signs over the huge garage before the overhead door thudded shut behind them: City Taxi Comapny. There was a hustle as the driver detached from the power source. Hero's door was yanked open and he was pulled out, and it was only then he realized that a small child had been huddled on the floor in back and was being hastened away.

"Ey, bub. Big Operator wants to see you in the terminal office." The cabbie jerked his head to the left, and then drove off. A man in uniform motioned Hero toward a glassed-in office.

The next thing he knew, his wrist was being clasped in the Ranger way. "Well, son. Most Rangers infiltrate Enchanted City as subtly as possible. The whole town knows you've arrived, not to mention the powers that be in the Dagoda. But welcome to the Resistance. We are all King's men and women here, working for the Restoration."

Hero's mouth dropped, and Big Operator smiled.

"Yessir, the dispatchers had themselves a job getting you out of that tight spot. It's not easy moving a taxi vanguard into position on a moment's notice.

"By the way, I think we picked up most of the orphans. That scattering tactic was pretty effective. The Resistance can use a man like you. How would you like to see the rest of the operation?"

The two walked to the middle of the taxi terminal, a large underground cavern with a huge map of Enchanted City on one wall. Big Operator pointed to the section that was Moire Oxan. "The Enchanter puts most of the heat

here. The people are poor and helpless, without wealth to barter for protection. As you know, orphans are taken to the Orphan Keeper and then put to work in the underground or on street crews."

Big Operator pointed to purple paper flags stuck all over the map. "Sightings," he explained. "The King has been sighted all over the city. The Enchanter's nervous—what with that and power outs. Shortages don't bother the City Taxi Company—ha-ha! We've developed our own solar storage cells so we can hook up or detach. Never trust man-made power. But our informants say the Dagoda's been a hot place with a whole lot of fire flying."

The terminal thrummed with the rumble of taxi engines, ignitions starting, tires squealing, doors banging. Big Operator lifted his voice.

"We have taxis posted all over the city. Those folks are dispatchers." He pointed to an electronic panel, where busy people wearing headsets monitored instruments. Hero noticed one dispatcher who seemed to be little more than a boy. "They keep tab on hot spots, send cabbies out on rescue sorties, whisk orphans off to Great Park if at all possible, and monitor Sightings."

Suddenly Hero remembered the cabbie who had taken him to the edge of the garbage heap when he had escaped from Enchanted City so long ago. He had thought then the driver had shouted, "To the King!"

Walking through a huge open door, Big Operator waved to a grease monkey, a woman wearing overalls. "Hey, Mac!" Hear we had a little action this morning." Then to Hero: "This is the garage. Maintenance crews overhaul taxis, keep them in running condition, wash them down. The Enchanter has a fleet of fancy limousines, but I'll take a swift little Resistance taxi in top-notch condition any day."

Hero's mind would not stop whirling. He didn't know which question to ask first. "But—but what about the Enchanter? How do you get by with this in the middle of Enchanted City?"

Big Operator smiled, but it was a grim expression. He put his arm around the lad's shoulders. "Make no mistake. The Enchanter is evil and he's dangerous—never forget it. The closer the Restoration, the more Sightings of the King—the more dangerous and desperate he will become." Then his smile became almost cocky. "But the truth is, the Enchanter only has power over those who fear him. Here in the Taxi Resistance, we are subjects of the King. Consequently, we are not afraid."

Hero looked straight ahead at a wall placard that read: SIGHTERS ARE NOT AFRAID! Big Operator studied his heroic troublemaker.

"Now, what are we going to do with you? You can't hear it in this underground terminal, but right now the death drums are beating out an all-points description on you. When the city wakes, you are going to be one wanted man. I don't dare make you a cabbie; that scar's too obvious. Last week, I needed a first-rank dispatcher, but a new recruit arrived who seems to have an in-born instinct for operations."

Big Operator walked over to the dispatcher's panel and checked a few notes that had been collected on clipboards. "Wait a minute; I think I have an idea. Hm-m-m-m-m-m. Little risky, but you're not without courage. I need to get you out of the terminal in case of raids. Stay right here."

Hero stood by the dispatchers' board, still amazed by his rescue and the turn of events. What kind of job would demand courage? He thought of the death drums beating out his description for the second time in his life. This unfortunate scar. He would've liked being a cabbie.

The dispatchers efficiently took messages and gave commands. "Zone-five, zero-o: twenty-twenty's in the ready and can make pick-up steady."

What command they brought to their job! They monitored the whole city; they made crucial life-saving decisions. He would've also liked to have been a dispatcher working for the Restoration.

He watched the back of the boy, the new recruit, who appeared quick minded, able, pausing to ask a question now and then. Leaning closer to the board, Hero thought: *How exciting to receive word of a Sighting! How could anyone be afraid who kept seeing the King?*

Without realizing it, Hero crowded the boy. The lad turned, looked up at him, and said, "Watch it! You're stepping on my gown!"

The voice was familiar; even the words had been spoken before. It was no boy at all. It was the Princess Amanda and as impertinent as ever: "I thought the idea was to infiltrate quietly, to be ready when the King needed us—not to draw attention to the Resistance by announcing oneself to all Enchanted City and making one royal nuisance of oneself!"

Hero was so glad to see her that he only laughed in amazement. "What are you doing here?"

"The same thing you're doing here," she retorted. "Working for the Restoration. Only I'm doing it a little more quietly." And with that she turned back to the board.

Amazed, Hero folded his arms, waiting for his assignment. He still wanted to ask hundreds of questions, but the dispatchers were frantically busy—getting orphans to safety, no doubt. He thought about his recent battle, of the shouted Names and the fresh rush of courage and the swinging hatchet. And he felt good. Maybe he was a hero after all, though a foolhardy one. Not only had he rescued one child; he had rescued many. Yes, sir!—that was worth a trip back to Enchanted City.

Suddenly cocksure, he stretched out his hand and knocked Amanda's cap to the floor; then he yanked on the braid that tumbled down her back. She yelped, turned toward him, and warned, "Remember, I have perfect aim!" And all the dispatchers stopped their work to look at her.

Quietly indeed, Hero thought to himself.

So Hero waited for his new assignment with fresh hope and renewed courage, not caring how dangerous the task. He was no longer alone, but surrounded by a great and adventurous company— the Taxi Resistance. True friends were near. In fact, he suspected that the Kingdom was all around him, if he but cared to find it.

33

The Challenger

*Big Operator gave the lad with the scar an unlikely
assignment: Keeper of the Chronicle of
Sightings of the King. The chief of the Taxi Resistance knew
that those who look harder for what they seek
often find more than they expect.*

"On-street sightings!" shouted Hero. "But—but I'm terrible at Sightings! I could hardly find the King in disguise in Great Park! How am I going to find him here in Enchanted City?"

Big Operator sat behind his desk in the glassed-in office of the City Taxi Company garage. "You can't stay here," he said. "Raids make your presence dangerous to us all. On the street you can be mobile, and the taxi brigade can keep you out of danger."

"But what about my scar? All of the Enchanter's men have a description of me by now. You yourself said there was a manhunt."

Big Operator was not to be moved. "I need an operator with street savvy and Ranger training. It's imperative that someone keep records of the King's activities. Hide your scar. Stay away from lights. The weather's turning cool; wear a scarf. Of course, this is a dangerous assignement. If you're afraid . . ."

Hero started to say that it wasn't fear, but at that moment the buzzer in the terminal sounded the yellow alert, indicating that a taxi was approaching in haste. A mechanic began to crank up the great garage door. At the same moment, a dispatcher at the control panel shouted, "Sighting!" The King had made himself known somewhere in the city. With amazement, Hero and Big Operator watched two frightened children climb confusedly out of the back of the cab. The door slammed; an echo reverberated.

"Hey!" shouted the driver. "I left the King t'bring dese kids in—but the Enchanter's car's comin'! Better get back to action." The cabbie indicated the location of the Sighting to a monitor, "Heraldry post 101; Moire Oxan." A pin was immediately stuck in the map of Enchanted City.

"Wait a minute!" cried Big Operator, turning to the lad. "What do you say, Hero? I need a chronicler right now out on the street. Do you want to see the King in action? The taxi can take you back."

To see the King—at that moment Hero forgot all his doubts. He clasped Big Operator's wrist in the Ranger way, grabbed his bag, and hurried to hop into the front seat of the taxi.

Amanda turned from the control board, shoved back her headset and earphones, and called, "Where are you going?"

Hero slammed the taxi door shut. The cabbie gunned the motor as the mechanic began to crank up the great door again. Hero leaned out the window and grinned. "To the streets. I'm going to see the King!"

Amanda stood at her seat. She seemed to have grown taller. "Be careful—" she started to say, and then stopped. "To the King!" she shouted. "To the Kingdom!"

The taxi was back out on the streets, squealing its brakes around corners and through narrow alleys. "King could be in big trouble. Sighted all over da city. Enchanter's not gonna like heralds vacating posts."

"How long will this cab keep running if it's not connected to the power line?" Hero asked.

The cabbie kept his eyes on his driving, but a smile cracked his stern face. "You mean, 'how long'll dis cab run if it *is* connected to the power line?' " It was an old driver joke. Power outs frequently disabled city transportation. "Kid— Big Operator's a genius. Storage cells keep taxis running with power lines or without. Yessir! Gonna live in da light."

Hero leaned back into the taxi seat. What in the world was he doing out on these streets? How would he live? Could he sight the King? The last words the King had spoken to him at the Great Celebration had been in reply to his own question: "How will I find you in Enchanted City? Will you be in disguise?"

Hero could remember the love in the young man's eyes. He saw again the richness of the royal garments, the gold glint in his hair; he heard the joyful camaraderie of the subjects of the King. The King had laughed and firmly clasped his hand. Hero could feel the warmth of that touch even now. He could hear the King saying, "That's right. You were never very good at Sighting. But it won't be hard for you to find me. I will have a scar just like yours."

The taxi slowed and dimmed its lights. Hero's stomach suddenly constricted. The long, black limousine of the Enchanter was parked by the curb. A group of people were gathered on the street within the glow of its headlights. Hero could hear herald horns blowing and the faint *din . . . din . . . din . . .* of the death drums beating. Great darkness was all around.

"Get out here," whispered the cabbie. "An all-point's bulletin is calling the vangard to action. Stay in d'shadows. King's in the middle."

Reluctantly, Hero left the security of the little taxi and slung his carryall over his shoulder. He crept into the shadow of a wall where no night-lights were shining. He could clearly see the group of people and the Enchanter standing on the curb, his cloak of woven wizardry flashing light and flame in the dark. It was the first time Hero had seen the evil ruler since his mother's death, though he had dreamt about him often enough in restless sleep.

The fire wizard stomped in rage on the pavement. "Who do you think you are? Insurrector! Rebel! Miscreant!" His voice rose in a crescendo of fury.

Hero crept closer, despite the danger. He wanted to see the man in the middle who was hidden by the crowd.

A calm voice answered. "I am the King. I am the true ruler of this city. The time for the restoration of my kingdom is at hand."

"HAH!" screamed the Enchanter. He stamped his feet and lifted his hands into the air. His fingers shot sparklers of fire. "HAH!" The wizard's eyes turned a malignant yellow. "To the Burning Place with you." Enchanter's men, Breakers and Burners, parted the crowd with cruel cudgels and hot glowing pokers and closed in on the figure in the center. "I'll teach you to defy me and tell tales of another Kingdom!"

At last Hero could see the man in the middle —but it couldn't be, it wasn't—was it? Compared to the Enchanter, with his flashing fire and robes moving like crimson flame, the man was ordinary, plain, unkinglike. Not at all like Hero's memories. He was dressed in common clothes. There was nothing glorious about him, nothing royal.

The challenger locked glances with the Enchanter. "This is not the time for burning. One day, I will break all your enchantments. For now, know that I have returned from exile!"

"*Ee-yi-yi-yi-yi—*" the Enchanter started to scream, "*yi-yi-yi-yi-*!!" It seemed as though his fury would crack the foundation of the city. "Your kingdom!" he spat with scorn. "Your kingdom is nothing but a few trees and a handful of dying outcasts and starving orphans!"

The taxi honked twice. HARNK-HARNK!—untrue! Hero moved close enough to see the faces of the combatants. Doubt and hope wrestled. The King could be in disguise. And no ordinary man could overcome the power of the Enchanter.

"My kingdom is here. It is anywhere I am and where my people obey my words." A taxi horn honked once. HARNK—true!

The Enchanter let forth a blast of flame that struck like a wall. The challenger lowered his head, crouched, and stumbled backward. Though his clothes were singed, he himself seemed to be unburned.

The Enchanter jeered, "Taste what I can do to insurrectionists! How about another blast? And another? And another?" Flames shot forth again and again, battering the man against the stone wall beside which Hero hid. Herald horns blew, one after another, and heralds cried, "Treason! Insurrection!" Naysayers sang their song of doom. *Nay-nay-nay; nay-nay-nay.*

This can't be the King, thought Hero. *A true king would never take such abuse. He must be a pretender.*

The crowd was slinking fearfully away into the shadows of the night. Someone had to do something. Hero started to unsheath his hatchet—then he heard the man shout, "No! This is not the time or the place!"

The challenger pushed himself away from the stones. He straightened his back, walked directly to the Enchanter, and again looked him straight in the eye, a long and unfaltering look. "Your enchantment is coming to an end, Evil One. Think on that. Tremble." Deliberately, he turned his back, limping from the effects of the fire battering, and walked away into the shadows of the street.

As he passed by, Hero had a good look at the man's face. *There was no scar.* The mans' face was smooth, unmarked. Proof. It couldn't be the King.

That's why there were no heroics—no war of flames, no vanquishing of the evil Enchanter in a moment of battle glory. The man wasn't the King. The whole Taxi Resistance had been fooled, duped. They wanted the Restoration so badly they were willing to believe any self-proclaimed deluder.

Then Hero realized that the Enchanter did nothing, that they were all enfolded in a powerful, unearthly silence. No more the rush of flame, no more the beating death drums, no more the song of the Naysayers. The Burners and Breakers stood like stone. The whole city seemed to be listening in a hushed and terrible quiet. The challenge rang in Hero's mind—*"I have returned from exile. . . . My kingdom is here."*

Hero heard a car door open and close, a motor accelerate, and then the sound of an engine fading down the street. Suddenly he knew he was standing alone in the presence of the Enchanter in the bone cold night air. He quickly covered his cheek with his hand, pulled his collar up around his neck, and started to creep away.

"Scarboy!"

Too late.

"Scarboy!"

Hero stopped. He waited for a cudgel blow to the head, a burning poker in his back. He expected the death drums to paralyze his soul, the song of the Naysayers to strike terror in his heart—but the strange silence continued, except for the old name, spoken by the old enemy.

Hero refused to turn around and look at the fire wizard. One look and he would be under the power of his evil eye. Did he have any power himself? Fool! How could one lad withstand the Enchanter?

The hatchet! Hero grasped the handle—but the man had said it wasn't time and *he* had walked away from this confrontation. Amazing! The man had been blasted by flames but not burned. *Your enchantment is coming to an end. Think on that . . . tremble.* If he was the King, he had chosen not to use his power. Was there danger to power used the wrong way at the wrong time? Hero released his grip on the hatchet handle.

"Scarboy!" The ugly voice called again.

Again Hero refused to turn around. Wait—wait! The challenger had looked the Enchanter in the eye, twice. *Who had ever looked the Enchanter in the eye and not been seared?* Nothing had happened! Except this silence. Maybe it was as dangerous for an enchanter to look a king in the eye as it was for him, Hero, to gaze at the Enchanter.

Then he heard it. The sound rose unbidden from some distant place, the one-note sound of the Rite of Adoption; flutelike, faint, faraway. *H-m-m-m-m-m-m-m,* it began. One lonely sound.

"SCARBOY!" the Enchanter shrieked, calling the old name frantically, as though he sensed power diminishing.

Little time; soon the silence would be broken. The one note hum swelled, filling his heart, beating wildly beneath his breastbone, gladdening his ear.

That was it! He might be scarred, but he was Scarboy no longer. He didn't belong here, in this evil place, this city doomed by enchantment. His home was Great Park, the King's place. His people were the people of Great Park—Mercie and Caretaker were his true parents.

Hero began to walk. Without looking back, without yielding himself to the eyes of the wizard who called his name, he walked to the beat of the hymn in his own heart. He no longer belonged here. The power of evil over him *was* diminished. He hurried down the street into the shadows, where the waiting taxi beeped one toot. Hero climbed into the front seat.

"Nice work," said the cabbie.

Hero relaxed against the seat and took a deep breath. *Nice work.* He almost laughed. He was a blunderer, he blundered into everything—danger, safety, friendship, conflict. The two watched as the Enchanter's car backed down the street, turned the corner, and disappeared. The place of confrontation was empty. Even the herald had deserted his post.

Something more tremendous than a War of Flames had just taken place. It took as much strength for a powerful man to choose *not* to use power as to use it—maybe more.

"Let's go," Hero said to the cabbie.

"Where to?" asked the driver, turning on the motor.

"To find the King, of course."

So Hero became the Keeper of the Chronicle of Sightings of the King. He was often in dangerous places, often filled with doubt; but he found more reason to believe than not to believe and he discovered for himself that in the Kingdom, where the King rules, believing is seeing.

The Most Beautiful Player of All

The Dagoda of the Enchanter loomed in the middle of Enchanted City, so that none would forget the watching eye of the fire wizard. Close by, and a happier place was the Palace of Players. Here the people of the city, filled with weariness and heartsickness, came and forgot for a time their griefs and fears and pains.

Thespia stood in the wings of the stage brushing her long and luxuriant hair. She was the most beautiful of all the players and even now she could hear the house chanting her name. "Thespia! We want Thespia!" Many suiters sought her hand, but she turned them all away.

"Flowers from the Dagoda!" the assistant stage manager called. Thespia yawned and instructed that the gift be delivered to her suite in the Palace.

"Four minutes! Four minutes!" the callboy warned. Thespia straightened her gown and took one last look in the mirror.

Through a crack in the thick velvet curtain, she could see that the theater was full. It was almost time for the play to begin. *Poor ones. Poor, poor ones. Forget for a while, then home again only to remember your empty half-lives.* She whispered this hollow blessing over them.

"See you t'night," the lead actor shouted as he hurried to take his position. "QUIET!" warned the stage director.

"But . . ." Thespia wanted to protest to the actor; then she shrugged her shoulders and turned to wait for that always-thrill, the curtains rising and the stage filling with the sudden radiance of spotlights, then the sonorous voices of trained players. She particularly loved tonight's play. *The Return of the King* had been banned for years, but recently several very old myth cycles had been restored to the Palace repertoire.

We need a king—Thespia quickly looked around as though the stagehands could read her innermost mind. Treason, this thinking; she knew it. Careful, or the most beautiful player of all could play a final role tied to a stake at Burning Place. The first rule all children of Enchanted City learned after branding was: THERE IS NO SUCH THING AS A KING. DEATH TO PRETENDERS!

Senseless! she thought, and looked around again. If there's no such thing as a king, why such a fuss? The placards, the lectures, the propaganda songs—". . . no king, no king, the Enchanter's the thi-ng." Silence would have helped her to forget, but each protest made her wish all the more: *If only there really were a king!*

"Three minutes! Three minutes!"

As a lonely understudy, Thespia had determined to be the finest player in all Enchanted City. Unlike the other actresses, who became arrogant and haughtily cut all ties with their pasts, Thespia perfected her art in the streets. She refused to become enamored with the sterile practice rooms, the posh living suites, and the luxuries of the Palace of Players. She bound up her flaxen hair with common cloth and walked the marketplace, listening to how real people spoke words.

Often she went back to her own people, to Moire Oxan where they lived, to the stacked hovels where she had been raised. There she carried old grannys' burdens that weighed their bent backs double and she brought tidbits of food for the always-hungry waifs. She wept when orphans were taken away to the Orphan Keeper and she felt the cold whistling through these always night lives, and remembered what it was to never have enough fire or power.

Their pain became her own, and their small and meagre joys as well. Because she did not despise them, she was loved: and it was they, the street people sitting on the gallery floor, who called her name.

One night, one terrible night, her cousin's wee babe wriggled in agony in Thespia's arms while searchers hunted its mother who was foraging in a city-edge workshift. It squinched up its tiny face, took a last, long breath, and died.

Shuddering with sobs, Thespia hid in a tower of the Players' Palace. How could she act the next night, play the comic, with this terrible knowledge—that babies died who shouldn't die in Enchanted City. She grieved with new understanding—there was little she, or anyone, could do.

Placards in the tower proclaimed: IT IS FORBIDDEN TO WATCH THE DAY. Her bitter soul declared: *Another ridiculous rule. I will watch the day—and if it slays me, then I am slain!*

As the golden sun rose, burning her eyes with grandeur and casting a brilliance over Enchanted City, Thespia thought she had never seen anything so beautiful. That moment of magnificent beauty marked her soul as truly as the branding iron had marked her body. *There must be more,* she thought. *This beautiful light must mean there is a better life.*

This was the moment she resurrected whenever she stepped onstage, whether it be for ordinary performances or for gala premiers or for command entertainments at the Dagoda—the light rising, shining gloriously over the city. That memory filled her with a special power.

In time Thespia had become what she had vowed to be—the greatest player of all. The simplest twist of her wrist, a motion of her hand, the arch of her eyebrows, one half-turn of her slender waist, left audiences amazed and delighted.

Thespia took deep breaths to calm her familiar stage anxiety.

"Orchestra and beginners!"

There was a backstage scurry as actors and actresses took their positions—stage left, stage center front—then a pounding, the one-minute signal, then the houselights dimming, then a hush as the audience quieted, then the lovely melody of an ancient hymn as the violins began their lilting music. Thespia loved the words of this overture.

> "Let us go down, go down
> and clasp hands
> and breathe life
> and taste the jagged edge of pain
> and sing songs of the better place,
> the better time,
> the better day."

No wonder she had fallen in love. For too long Thespia had watched the Breakers cudgel men and women in Moire Oxan; for too long she had heard

the chilling moan of the Naysayers in the wind of winter's night—*nay-nay-nay, nay-nay-nay, nothing-can-be-done, nothing-will-be-done, nay-nay-nay.* Thespia had fallen hopelessly in love with the King.

Oh, not the actor/king (though he was handsome and her ardent admirer), but the mythical king of the play—the one who was strong but not brutal, who could laugh with joy and weep with freedom, who never leered at beautiful women, who told stories to children and gentled the fears of the old, whom the young men followed because he was the bravest of all, who found beauty in the ugly, and whose very words spoke hope.

So the flowers wilted, the love suits went unanswered, and Thespia convinced all in the Dagoda that she was passionately devoted to her art alone. And every time she acted in *The Return of the King,* it was like falling in love all over again.

"P-s-s-s-t, Thespia," the prompter hissed. "Entrance!"

She stepped onto the stage, her hair tumbling in captured stagelight, glowing like a halo. There was a gasp from the gallery and applause from the boxes. She closed her eyes and evoked the memory of the roseate sun, rising, rising—and stood shimmering beneath the overhead spotlights. "Oh, we are mortals and have forgotten how to laugh. Who will show us where laughter is hiding?" Thespia's lashes glistened with tears because it was true, so true.

Perhaps Thespia's power came from the gallery, from the men and women and children sitting on the floor and wearing ragged, tattered clothes. They, too, wondered where the laughter had gone. Most players acted to the boxes, to the rich patrons dripping with furs, sitting in plush chairs, their stomachs full. But Thespia played to the floor, to the people. She looked at them with pity. Eager, the whole mob lifted their heads to the stagelight, their mouths open, their eyes wide with wonder.

Thespia loved to make them laugh, loved their unsophisticated whooping, howling, and floor pounding. She loved to make them weep, to spill the overflow of sorrow that became dammed in the dark horrors of Enchanted City.

Tonight beyond the circle of reflected stagelight, she thought she saw a man standing, but he was in the gallery shadow. *Strange. Why don't the ushers have him sit or leave?*

Two stage beats, a pause. At this moment, the actor/king stepped from the wing. This was one of the play's dramatic moments, the actual return of the King; but suddenly, the lights flickered and dimmed. A groan went up from the theater.

"Power out! Oh-h-h-h-h-h. Power out!"

Even the players on stage moaned.

"Lights! Lights! Lights!" shouted the street people.

"Doesn't anything ever work in this wretched city!" In dismay Thespia realized she had spoken out loud. The actor/king leaned close to her, *"Careful! Rumors say there's revolt underfoot."*

But then Thespia realized that a light *was* shining in the darkened auditorium. The man she had seen in the gallery shadow seemed to be standing in his own light. She gasped and took a closer look; he seemed vaguely familiar. From the back of the hall, he raised his hand in greeting. Shyly, hardly realizing she did so, she reached out her hand toward him.

And the theater quieted as all watched the man walk within a center of radiance to the orchestra pit. He perched upon the rim, apologized to the musicians, and vaulted up to the stage. "This is where I make my entrance, I believe," he said, and his voice was wonderful, filled with the echo of faraway hills and laughing country streams.

He stood in the middle of the stage and held out strong arms. "There is a real kingdom," he announced, "and a real king."

Without knowing that they moved, all the players took one step closer to his warmth. Some in the gallery rose to their knees.

The man motioned to the conductor. "Music," he said, and the orchestra began to play. "Up tempo." The beat quickened in the percussion section and wound its way in and out among the street people whose feet began to tap.

"In the Kingdom of Light, there is no night."

And the man smiled at the gallery, at all in the house and at the players onstage. The beat waltzed its way to the tiers of boxes, and even a few of the wealthy patrons began to clap: *Ta-dum-ta-dum-ta-da-da-dum.*

"In the Kingdom of Light," the man chanted, "the day shines bright."

The music was infectious. Now many chanted back, "In the Kingdom of Light, the day shines bright."

Ta-da-ta-da-ta-da-da-dum, played the orchestra. The man raised his hands for quieter music.

"Have you ever heard of a kingdom where outcasts were welcomed?" the man asked.

And the people answered, "No-o-o-o-o!"

"Have you ever heard of a kingdom where every orphan had a home?"

"No-o-o-o-o-o-o-o!"

"Or where those who loved light could live in it? Or where those who sought for a king found him?"

The man lowered his voice to a stage whisper, and the whole audience leaned forward to hear, "In the Kingdom of Light, everything's right!"

Ah-h-h-h-h-h-h-h, sighed the house. And for a moment, everyone in the audience knew this was no play, no myth cycle dragged out of the palace archives. *"Ah-h-h-h-h-h-h,"* sighed the gallery again, a long sigh. If only there were such a place, such a real place.

The man offered his arm to the actor-king standing on one side of him and his other arm to Thespia who also stood near. She looked out on the audience and gasped—the people in the gallery were clothed in warm garments, their runny sores were healed, they were clean and healthy. This couldn't be true. She blinked her eyes and stared again and realized she was seeing the people through the glow of the man's light.

Tears ran down her cheeks, real tears, not player's tears. If it could only be; if there really were such a place. "Wh-wh-who are you?" she asked, and he answered, "You know who I am." Sobs broke her words. "But h-how do w-we find this kingdom of w-which you speak?"

He turned, took both her hands in one hand, and wiped away her tears. The other players gathered close, and one put his arm around Thespia's shoulders to comfort her.

"Follow me," said the man. "The real kingdom is wherever I walk and whenever anyone walks with me."

Thespia knew. He was wearing common clothes, the plain garments of the people, but she wanted to fall at his feet and bow. Tears blurring her vision, she turned from the man, faced the audience, and walked to the edge of the stage. She stretched one hand to him and one hand to the gallery, as if in introduction. "The King," she said. "My Lord, the people."

Suddenly, the lights blinked off-on; the man-made power was coming up. Someone in the boxes shouted: THERE IS NO SUCH THING AS A KING! DEATH TO PRETENDERS! And several began to chant: DEATH! DEATH!

The orchestra stopped playing and all the notes tumbled together and fell in a heap, and the man-made power suddenly came fully on and the lights blazed forth. The audience shifted in their seats and patted their clothes straight. What a strange play—it must be intermission—but then all these old myth cycles were odd. They stood to stretch. And the magical moment was gone and the players exited, trying to remember what lines had been said and which lines remained to be said and who had the last cue; and the stage director didn't know which act to call next.

But Thespia stayed beside the man, who was buttoning his coat as though he meant to go. "Are you leaving?" she asked.

"Yes, the moment for believing is gone."

She held her breath. "C-can I come with you?"

He bowed and took her hand and kissed it; then he helped her climb as gracefully as possible over the orchestra pit, and they walked down the aisle and left the theatre together. And very few seemed to see them go.

And Thespia became a street player in the back alleys
and dead ends of Enchanted City, acting out the King's story
in such a way that all who saw her suspected—then hoped—that
there was a real kingdom. Like the King, she worked in common
clothes, and she never gave the luxuries of the Palace a
backward glance, because when one has found one's real love it is
easy to leave what has only been pretend.

The Sewer Rat
And the Boiler
Brat

Deep beneath Enchanted City, great sewers rushed wastewater to treatment centers where sludge and gases were separated and then piped to the enormous boiler room for burning. Here huge vats of boiling water spewed steam through underworld tubes, creating man-made power. Sewer rats and boiler brats, the orphans who manned this underworld, dreaded power outs more than cold, more than hunger because then the merciless rage of the Enchanter's men fell on them.

The filthy drainage rushed through the great sewers. Sewer Rat No. 1 sniffed the air; he had lived in this underworld for so long he could smell a backed-up drain a mile away. In the dark, he inched along the narrow walkway above the reeking wastewater, heading for drain 75S.

Achooee! he sneezed. He had been a sewer rat ever since he could remember, and he always had a cold. Boiler Brat, his best and only friend, talked of "up-there." Up-there were city lights and warm fires and mothers and fathers. Sewer Rat No. 1 had no memory of up-there. His forever memory was of the dark and the damp. He thought he had never really been warm—*Achooee!* As far as he knew, his mother was the rank sewer and his father was the sound of rushing wastewater—*shloosh-shu.* The only memory that was not of down-here was the sound of a lone clear note, haunting to Sewer Rat No. 1. He couldn't remember the rest of the tune and he didn't know where it came from—just one note sounding from far, far away.

"Dis-here's the drain," he shouted into the cavern of the huge sewer pipe. "Ay-yo, sewer rats! Dis-here's the drain! Sebenty-five-south! Ay-yo, sewer rats! Drain sebenty-five south!"

Other boys and girls crept through the darkness, all miserable sewer rats like himself, orphans taken into the Enchanter's custody at their parents' deaths with no one to love them, no one to protect them, no one to make them wash. They were dirty faced, ragged, ill-mannered and snotty nosed. Some rats inched cautiously along the walkways—newcomers who remembered up-there. Others ran in confident abandon, their bare feet and hands acting like suctions against the damp dripping sewer walls or on the network of treatment pipes that crisscrossed the stinking hollow of the underworld cavern.

Sewer Rat No. 1 shouted orders: "Lower 'em down dere now. Don't swallow nutt'n. Hurry 'em up, youse sewer rats!"

Three boys and two girls holding grappling hooks were lowered by others into the wretched waters. Sewer Rat No. 1 scrambled to turn the huge valve that shut the drain. No use losing good workers in the suck-up, the powerful rush of waters that occurred once the drain was unclogged. After a few moments, the five broke the surface, grasping for breath. Instantly, five others dived in.

"Hey-ya! Hey-ya!" cried Sewer Rat No. 1. "Dat blasted siren's gonna go—den we got d'Breakers on our backs."

Suddenly, an awful wailing shriek began. The sound of it bombarded the sewer caverns, violently sloshing the wastewater. A bubble trap!—a giant air pocket—had formed during the hasty opening and closing of the main valve. Now the steam in the boiler room would shut down, and all Enchanted City would plunge into darkness.

A little girl beside Sewer Rat No. 1 screamed, "Power-out! Power-out. Oh-oh-oh! They'll get us now. Now we'll get it."

Sewer Rat No. 1 hushed her; Rat No. 72, too small to be down-here—she hadn't even undergone branding. But little rats could climb into minor clogged pipes and drains. He took her hand as she cried and roughly swung her to his shoulder. "Well, rats, we'se in for it. All of youse, follow me." His voice could hardly be heard above the siren wail.

With heavy hearts, sewer rats dropped from the pipes to which they had climbed, their bare feet padding against the wet walkways.

"Oh-ooh-oh," the little girl moaned, clutching Sewer Rat No. 1's head.

"Shadya mout," he whispered gruffly. He knew her crying would incite the Breakers.

The children gathered in the boiler room. The angry maws of the furnace doors were open, waiting for more fuel, but the great grim boilers were beginning to sputter and spout, shutting down because of the bubble trap. Boiler brats were throwing down their sludge shovels and taking off their hard hats. With dread, they watched Breakers already slipping around the iron cauldrons and the maze of blast pipes. These grim shadows crept silently into the darkening power station. The children all knew there was no one who could keep them safe.

Sewer Rat sniffed death. These were the no-people who had given themselves to the Enchanter, and now they had no minds but to do the work of the evil ruler. In the dim light, their chalky-white faces set off piercing black eyes full of malice. All held cudgels, brutal clubs with ugly knobs, in their folded arms.

The huge boilers gurgled and bubbled hopelessly as one by one they shut down.

"Ma-ma, ma-ma," wept a little child, very quietly.

"Full-scale power out! Flum-ba!" said a boy wearing a suit of heatsease, flimsy metal-like material that sometimes shielded brats from fire and steam. "Oh, flum-ba, someone's gonna get it!" It was Boiler Brat No. 1, Sewer Rat's friend, and these two felt responsible for all the other children.

"Ay-yo, someone gonna get broke if someone don' do somtin' fast."

"You gonna pop the bubble?" Boiler Brat challenged.

Popping the bubble: it meant diving down to the drain with the valve open, finding the air pocket, piercing it and hanging on for dear life as swooshing wastewater exploded through the open drain. Swimming back was sure doom. A popper could only hope by claw or by gnaw to catch the next downpipe drain. One rat had survived popping, but he was pretty blasted and he swallowed so much filthy water that he later died of sewer poisoning.

Suddenly, the Boiler Room was filled with fiery light. The Enchanter himself had emerged from an opening, as a herald's voice cried, "The Fire Wizard, Lord of the Death Drums, God of the Fire Priests, Commander of Burners and Breakers and Naysayers!"

The children, sewer rats and boiler brats, edged toward the walls and tried to sneak behind pipes, only to be pushed back by the brutal clubs of the

Breakers. In a rage, the Enchanter was hot to the touch; those who came too close could be scorched.

Obviously infuriated, the man who loved fire lifted his red head and screamed, one heart-stopping shriek that pierced to the very soul of all the children, *"Ee-yi-yi-yi-yi-yi-yi-yi-yi-yi-yi-yi!"*

"Power outs! Power outs! How many times do I have to tell you power outs are forbidden in my kingdom? Someone's going to pay for this! Someone's going to pay plenty." Opening his hands, his fingers shot flames.

The rats and the brats cringed. By now the Enchanter was surrounded by his personal bodyguards, the Burners, their pokers flashing in the half-dark.

"Oh-ooh-oh," wailed a little voice. No. 72 was overcome with terror. "Oh-ooh-oh," her voice cried, getting louder and louder.

"Silence!" shouted the Enchanter. His voice boomeranged in the blast room. His flashing eyes were malignant. "Who dares to interrupt me?"

Sewer Rat No. 1 knew it was useless to explain that the noise was just one frightened little girl. Who in all Enchanted City cared about the trauma of an orphan child?

"Bring the offender here!" commanded the Enchanter. Instantly, Burners moved toward the wail. A Breaker raised a cudgel and jammed it against 72. She screamed in pain and fell in a clump. Roughly, Burners dragged her limp body to the Enchanter.

"Somebody's got to do something," whispered Boiler Brat No. 1.

"Silence!" shouted the Enchanter again. And all obeyed. Even No. 72 was silent. She had fainted in fear.

The tall fire wizard's voice grew sinister. "Ah-h-a-a-a-a, I think I have a solution. Firing. Firing for five. Who will walk through the flames? Any volunteers? Here's the first." He pointed to the child at his feet and laughed, *"Owa-ha-ha, Owa-ha-ha."*

Suddenly Sewer Rat No. 1 sneezed, *"Achooee!"*

The Enchanter looked at him through narrowed eye-lids. "Ah, Sewer Rat No. 1. Are you volunteer two?"

Sewer Rat No. 1 swallowed hard. He took one step forward. "Actually, Sire, hows about popp'n?"

A yellow light shone in the wizard's eyes, and the pokers in the hands of the Burners flashed brighter. "Ah, yes, popping. Any suggestions? Who's the lucky popper?"

Sewer Rat No. 1 sneezed again and pointed to himself. "Uh, Sire, here's

the man for d'job. No need for firin'. Right, Sire?"

The Enchanter raised his head and laughed. He laughed and laughed, sounding like a hyena howling over its prey. *"Owa-ha-ha; owa-ha-ha."* He stopped. "Oh, heroics. I love heroics. Why of course, Sewer Rat No. 1. Be hero of the day. Just get that bubble trap out of the drain. I don't care if No. 1 or No 101 dies doing it."

With that, a signal was given: the Burners surrounded the Enchanter and exited from the room, taking the fiery light with them. The Breakers kept guard, holding the sewer rats and boiler brats hostage to No. 1's intent, and the children huddled in a relieved panic in the dim shadows of the boiler room.

"Sewee," Boiler Brat whispered. "How's you gonna come out in one piece?" Sweat ran down his forehead.

"Don' know," said No. 1. "But d'bubble's gotta pop."

Sewer Rat No. 1 opened the valve above drain 75S. *Dese d'last—d'last dive, d'last moments.* And he shuddered as he thought of popping. He shuddered again as he thought about firing, about hostages forced to walk through the flames, and he was glad that No. 72 would be safe for a little while. But he would never see up-there. *What is up-there?* he wondered. *This underworld is bad, dark and cold. Is up-there good, bright and warm?*

Fear made No. 1 shiver all over. He sniffed the air—no one was near. He was glad that the other rats were held hostage and that no one could see him shaking. Boilee was good. *My friend Boiler Brat.* Sewer Rat No. 1 took a deep breath, lowered his head, prepared to plunge—when suddenly he smelled something.

Sewer Rat looked up. A soft glow filled the end of the tunnel beyond drain 75S. Burners? No, no. But a man, a stranger stood in the warm light. No. 1 thought he heard a note sounding from far away, clear, strong and haunting.

"What are you doing, No. 1?" the stranger called, standing on the walkway on the other side of the sewer tunnel.

"Poppin . . ."

"Hm-m-m-m. Risky business."

"Power out. Wizard's fired up. Know wha' that means?"

"Firing?"

"Ay-yo." Then Sewer Rat No. 1 sneezed. *"Achooee!"*

"In the Kingdom of Light, it's always right," said the man, and the one note seemed louder.

"A kingdom?" asked No. 1. His heart was beating rapidly

"Yes, a kingdom where the king is good and all the people live up-there and where every orphan belongs to somebody."

"Don' believe it."

The stranger started to hum the same one note. Then he stopped. "Don't pop."

"But firing—" Sewer Rat protested.

"Close the drain valve. Stack rocks from the sewer siding in the drain chute. Open the drain. The suck-up will force the rocks through the bubble trap. The Enchanter himself knows how popping can be done with no risk to life."

Sewer Rat No. 1 looked at the stranger in amazement—could this be true? He struggled to shut the valve. He grunted and pulled and heaved rocks from the siding across the work platform above drain 75S. They tumbled down the chute and smashed against the closed system. He rushed to the valve and strained to open it. A splash, a tumbling moan in the pipes, then a bursting pop! followed by a wooshing, turbulent swooshing of wastewater! It worked!

No. 1 scrambled across the network of tubes to the other side. He wanted to see this stranger up close. He wanted to be near his light. He wanted to be warm.

"How yo know 'bout dis?"

The stranger smiled, "I know much more. I care who dies, or who is afraid, or who is weeping, or who is without love."

The radiance from the stranger folded Sewer Rat No. 1 in warmth.

"Yo know dis note?"

"I know the whole song. Come follow me up-there and I will teach you the rest of the tune."

No. 1 hung his head. There was nothing in the world he wanted more than to leave this terrible underworld, to walk in the warmth of the light from this strange and wonderful stranger, to learn the rest of the notes of the one note that haunted his memory—but—but—

"But?"

Sewer Rat looked up into the eyes of the man. "But Boilee, m'fren, and No. 72, and all the rats and brats."

"Come with me," said the stranger, and the rat did. Together they climbed through the sewer world, over causeways and walkways and crisscross networks of pipes. The whole way the one note sounded above their heads, calling, calling. They came to the boiler room. The great vats had begun to heat—churning and bubbling and s-s-s-teaming. The Breakers had all gone, and the boiler brats were shoveling sludge again. The sewer rats sat in a sad circle, their heads hanging. None could bear to discover what had happened to No. 1.

"Sewee!" cried Boiler Brat No. 1 when he saw his friend. "You popped!" All the other children cheered and clapped. No. 72 ran to his side and embarrassed him with her hug.

"N'na. N'me," he stuttered and pointed to the stranger. "Him. He—"

It was then that the children really saw the stranger. And the one-sound note entered into the heart of each orphan child, no matter how dirty or ugly. *He is like my father,* each thought, *or my favorite older brother, or my best friend.* And none knew this was the thought of all the others. *I have heard that song, but what is the rest of the tune?* they wondered.

The boiler room, filled with ash piles and grime and mounds of furnace clinkers, was flooded with the stranger's soft light. For the first time the sewer rats and the boiler brats saw how dirty they were, how ragged and how forlorn. They wanted to be clean and sleep in warm places and have someone fuss over them and bring them good food.

"Come follow me," the stranger called. "Hum the one note you know, and I will teach you the rest of the music."

And the children hummed, the big tough boys and the rough girls and the tiny ones too young for branding—*m-m-m-m-m-m-m; m-m-m-m-m-m-m.*

"What about the Breakers?" Boiler Brat asked, but the stranger only smiled and hummed the note louder, and somehow they knew they would be safe with him. Sewer Rat No. 1 put his arm around his friend, Boiler Brat, and they all, every last one, followed the stranger out of the dark underworld.

And they marched after the man who reminded them all of
their fathers and they hummed the call of the one-tone tune,
out of the fetid underworld and the dangerous blast room,
through the city where all the people stared,
past the ashes of Burning Place, over the garbage heap
to a strange old gate, into a park where trees grew.
And no one stopped them because the stranger led them,
and they would have followed farther,
farther in order to be close to the only One who cared about tired,
lost, cold, hungry, and unhappy orphans.

The Forbidden Princess

*In the courtyard of a small temple on the same street
as the grand Dagoda of the Enchanter, the Forbidden Princess
came nightly to her balcony so that all who desired might gaze at her
beauty. She was beautiful, indeed, but her eyes
were empty and her expression blank.*

Oh, *Great Park . . . Great Park.* Amanda sighed and longed for her
friends, Caretaker and Mercie, remembering the Circle of Sacred Flames
and the Great Celebrations. How she would love to make entrance and
become real—a princess again.

Despite these longings, she contented herself to be doing the crucial work
of the Kingdom. In the months since slipping into Enchanted City, she had
learned respect for her unpolished compatriots in the taxi resistance and for the
skills of the chief, Big Operator, and she had discovered that her own gifts of
perfect aim and seeing were invaluable to the cause.

Amanda spent many nights in the little courtyard not far from the bustling
terminal of the City Taxi Company. She liked to sit in the soft light of the

courtyard lanterns and remember Great Park—the graceful wood doves, the forest creatures, the pattern of leaf and sun and shade on a hidden stream.

After a while, Amanda realized that the dark-skinned beauty who came to the balcony was not simply idling away the nights; she was appearing on command. Citizens came to the temple—one here, another there, perhaps two or three together—and turned their faces toward the balcony. A tiny bell rang, a mere whisper of sound, and then the girl would appear, her soulless eyes staring. "Ah," they would say. "Such beauty!"

At first, Amanda came to the courtyard simply because she needed a rest from the stress of traffic dispatching. Now she came because the plight of the girl drew her, a plight she didn't understand.

One night a damp fog stinking of sludge smoke and burning garbage settled on the city. Amanda walked the dark streets, restless for clean air and the sun and a romp on spongy moss. She was not afraid to roam at night. Amanda was not afraid of anything, except her own dangerous stubbornness—a lesson hard learned in a terrible incident which had brought shame to herself, pain to all she loved, and disaster to the only place she would ever call home.

She had loved a forbidden thing and had not been the same child since. A child with wild flowers in her hair, whose laughter constantly announced her presence, Amanda once had loved extravagantly, without question. Now she questioned all loves and was cautious about loving anything.

On this night Amanda slipped into the courtyard. The lanterns cast an eerie glimmer in the fog which oozed from the streets under the heavy outer doors. She stood beneath the balcony window, glad that the girl would not have to make many appearances on this frightful night.

The bell whispered—oh, dear, she had gazed too long. The girl appeared; Amanda was sorry to have disturbed her. "She's very beautiful," said a voice from the shadows behind her.

Amanda whirled around! Who was hiding in the courtyard?

"Don't be afraid—" the form moved away from the cloisters. Even in the damp fog, its motion was familiar. The voice was comforting, a well-known voice.

Her old impudence returned. "Have you nothing better to do than frighten unsuspecting maidens in dark streets? I thought you were supposed to be out chronicling Sightings." But Amanda was glad to see her old friend. Though she had heard much about his exploits, their paths had not crossed since that first day's encounter in the taxi terminal.

Hero spoke in a low voice. "The same old Amanda. Be careful what you say. Anyone (or anything) may be hiding in the shadows. This is a bastion of the Enchanter."

He lifted a lantern from its hook and carefully shone it in the corners. They were alone. The girl on the balcony had taken her bored silence inside.

He was taller than she remembered. By the light of the lantern she noticed that the planes and angles of his face had broadened, outgrowing the scar which had disfigured a boy's cheek. Now the old wound gave him a rakish, elegant air. He had become handsome.

She wanted to protest, "I'm *not* the same old Amanda. I'm no longer just a play friend!" But she suspected he had grown so tall he would never notice that she had grown as well.

He pulled her to a bench, where they sat together, "Big Operator told me that you come here often." He spread his dark blue slicker around her shoulders to shelter her from the damp. Its color reminded her of the soft, rich homespun of Ranger cloaks, of flashing silver insignias, of courage and proud command and of the forest cry, "The Kindgom comes!"

"Amanda, you need to be careful roaming through Enchanted City. Great dangers lurk in every corner of every street."

Amanda stiffened. Her answer was also low. "I can take care of myself."

But Hero was in earnest. "In Great Park you are the amazing princess who used to outspit and outaim any contenders! But this is my territory. Innocence is dangerous in Enchanted City. Case in point: Don't ever come out on rainy nights without a covering, some sort of macintosh. Even the air bodes ill; people die of the nightailment. The health you take for granted in Great Park, the healing powers of Mercie are not natural to this place."

Amanda felt an old indignation rise—she was not a child—but just as suddenly it slipped away. She had learned all too well the folly of arrogance. She *had* been cold. She *was* glad for the warmth of his shared rain cloth. He was right, the paths and forest trails were her native terrain; but the hard paving stones of this dark place were his. Now she must learn from him.

The courtyard doors to the street creaked open. A form crept in and Amanda felt Hero tense beside her and grasp the handle of the hatchet beneath his slicker. A Breaker had entered the courtyard. Amanda's own heart quickened; she had once seen the chalky white face, the piercing eyes, the chilling grin, the cudgel raised to bash her as she lay in pain. *To the King*, she mentally intoned. *To the Restoration*. The bell whispered; the girl came to the balcony; the Breaker gazed and withdrew to the streets.

Hero murmured again, "She's so beautiful even the no-people come to look."

"But her eyes, her eyes—they're blank. There's no life in them."

"Of course," explained Hero. "She's the Forbidden Princess."

"The Forbidden Princess?" Amanda asked. They were out on the street now, walking back to the Taxi Company.

City wise, the young man told her the story of the beautiful girls gathered together every year to serve as temple keepers for the Enchanter. Chosen for their courage as well as for their beauty, a terrible initiation separated those who were worthy from those who were only fair. The novitiates spent a night in a room with severed bulls' heads. Those who didn't weep or whine were chosen to become princesses who spent the rest of their young lives allowing the curious to gaze on their faces, but forbidden to speak to any admirers.

"How awful!" said Amanda.

"That's not all. Eventually they become wives to the Enchanter. The children they bear are the Enchanter's elite guard, Burners and Breakers, the no-people. The Enchanter has had thousands of wives. Most of them shrivel and waste away—heartsickness. His embrace is so terrible that even beauty and courage are not protection enough."

They stood talking before the overhead garage door of the City Taxi Company and waited for a cab to return rather than bother a mechanic. Sometimes, in the rain, the city was almost beautiful the way the lights danced on the wet stones. A taxi beeped its horn, the crank creaked inside, the door slid upwards.

"Amanda?" Hero placed a hand on her shoulder. "Don't go to the temple courtyard so often. It's dangerous. There's nothing you can do for the princess, and Big Operator says your work as a dispatcher is invaluable. Hundreds have been helped because of your quick gifts of seeing and aiming."

Amanda watched him stride off into the night, confident, his back broad. Nothing she could do! Nothing she could do! Then who would help the forlorn girl? But wait—wait, she had promised nothing. Hero had forgotten too much; *she* had once slayed a dragon singlehandedly in mortal combat. Hero's job was chronicling Sightings, who was to say her job wasn't the rescuing of forbidden princesses?

Amanda went back to the courtyard every night. She went at different times between control board duty, taking different alleys and streets, but she told no one because she was afraid they would forbid her—and Amanda had had enough pain from forbidden loves.

What would Mercie do in the city, with her powers confined by enchantment? she asked herself.

Each night when Amanda sat in the courtyard, she silently spoke the names of the King. Whenever the Forbidden Princess came to the balcony, Amanda closed her eyes, took sure aim, and with her powerful gift of seeing, pointed the names right at the girl's heart.

His Majesty . . . my Sovereign Liege Lord . . . His Eminence . . . the Benevolent Potentate . . . His Supreme Holiness . . . the Lord Monsiegneur . . . His Most Royal Highness . . . the Monarch of All . . . the true King . . . to Him and to the Restoration of His Kingdom!

As Amanda did her lonely work, she watched for the slightest flicker of life in the eyes staring from the balcony, but there was nothing. Guilty memory taunted her—*forbidden love, forbidden love.* Crucial concentration came hard. Then one night as she sighted inwardly, she was sickened by seeing the evil eye of the Enchanter, searching, darting to and fro—and Amanda understood she was in peril. She knew she should end her vigils, but there—

there! That very night, a tear dropped from the corner of the girl's eye. A sign of life! Amanda knew she had come again to love a thing dangerous to love.

So Amanda returned, hiding in the shadows of the cloisters, scarcely breathing lest she draw the ominous attention of the evil eye in the nearby Dagoda but aiming the Names from her heart to the heart of the girl standing on the balcony. At last, at last, the Forbidden Princess lifted her eyes as though wakening from a trance, and then turned her head toward the shadows as though peering for the silent speaker of the Names.

The girl had been awakened. The Names had done their life-giving work. Now, how to get her out before horror overtook them both? A plan! Slip into the courtyard, hide; then help the princess escape in the daylight, when the city was sleeping.

The next night Amanda left her earphones and headset hanging neatly on their hook, finished her dispatcher's notes, and crept without telling anyone into the little temple where she hid in the darkest corner. Finally, the gatekeeper turned the key in the outside lock. To her surprise she heard him say, *"She's locked inside."*

Which she? Amanda wondered. Her breath quickened. Eyes shut, looking inward, she was horrified to see the eye of the Enchanter looking straight at her! An evil smile lit up his face. Closing off sight, she hurriedly began the litany of names. This time, she spoke them aloud, urgently evoking the full sum of powers available to her.

"His Majesty the King!" The Forbidden Princess walked to the balcony. "My Sovereign Leige!" The girl leaned over the wrought iron, as Amanda herself walked boldly out of the shadows to the paving stones. "His Eminence!" The eyes of the Forbidden Princess filled with tears. "The Most Benevolent Potentate!" The tears splashed on the stones. "His Supreme Holiness!" The sky overhead began to shine slightly with a faint cast of dawn light. "The Lord Monsiegneur!"

The girl broke the silence and spoke, rather wept aloud hysterically, "It is too late—too late! Oh-oh-oh-oh! The Enchanter comes today to take me to the bridal chamber."

There was a pounding at the gate. BLAM! BLAM! BLAM! Amanda's heart failed. *Too late!* The distant echo of the death drums began to sound— *oom-bha-pah, oom-bha-pah*—calling sentries from the Dagoda to action.

What had she done? Awakened the princess out of her unfeeling numbness so she would be totally aware of the torture ahead? Placed her own valuable gifts of seeing and perfect aim as hostage to the enemy? These loves, these loves, these terrible loves! Would she never learn that love was dangerous? Why risk so much for one miserable girl among so many? Would she never learn about forbidden things?

The outer door—a key! Too late. The gatekeeper had returned.

Amanda drew herself to full stature and shouted the last names. "To the Monarch of All! To the King! To the Restoration of his Kingdom!" She knew she uttered treason and death was the penalty for her actions. But she was a princess of Great Park. Her heritage was of royal lineage; she would not whine or cry out or beg for mercy. For the sake of the King, she would march proudly to Burning Place.

Amanda held high her head as a man entered through the swinging gates.

He said, "Thank you, my sister. You honor me well." It was the King himself!

Amanda gasped. "But how? The locked latch—the key—" Through the open gates she could hear the death drums beating louder, faster.

"Did you forget that I can open all closed doors?"

He looked very plain. There were no golden highlights in his hair, his clothes were common—but the voice! It sounded of clear waters falling over great boulders, of winds blowing across fragrant fields. And the eyes! They contained the hush of the deep far sky itself, vast and infinite.

"Let us hurry to finish this work you have begun," he said, and he stepped beneath the balcony where the princess was weeping hysterically with her head hidden in her arms. "Beloved!" he called quietly. "My beloved!"

The girl raised her head, and her eyes grew wide and her weeping stopped. The voice of the One of the Names had spoken; she knew him instantly and reached out her hands in an appeal for rescue. Clambering up the vines to the balcony, the King quickly lowered the princess by her wrists to the courtyard stones.

"We are a little short of princesses right now where I come from," he explained gently after he himself had vaulted down. "They're all growing up and accomplishing great things in the world—"

He smiled at Amanda, the old, wonderful smile filled with kingslove, and for a moment it was as though they were in the Inner Circle surrounded by the dancing, leaping Sacred Flame. "And they are learning that because some loves are forbidden, not all loves are so."

Relief flooded Amanda. She bowed her knee in a courtly curtsey and murmured, "My Liege Lord."

Then, sheltering the frightened girl in his arms, he said, "I think you had better come and be a princess in the company of my people."

In short order, they piled into a waiting taxi. To Amanda's surprise, Hero was sitting in the front seat. He reached over, gave her hand a squeeze and said, "Good work," How wonderful to be fellow to a brigade that could arrange last-minute rescues!

Amanda glanced through the open doors of the empty courtyard as the taxi pulled away. She felt relief, but—but jauntiness, too. Some of the old spirit of field and stream and childhood returned. A girl had been rescued from a terrible fate and was now nestled in the embrace of the King. No one—not Hero, not the cabbie, nor His Majesty—had scolded her with a "What-in-the-name-of-Great-Park-possessed-you?"

She smiled back at Hero and was proud because *she* did not remind him that street wise, alley smart, he had said she could do nothing. It was true. She *had* done nothing. The Names and the King had done it all—but for a field child unused to city ways, she had done nothing very well indeed!

Nor did Amanda say, "I can take care of myself," because she was learning that old follies haunt prideful independence, and in the last breathless moments in that tiny courtyard, she had become utterly convinced that the work of the Restoration was best done in the company of worthy compatriots.

70

The Carnival Daughter

If the Enchanter looked into a child's eyes, his gaze could burn a scar on the soul. Some children became ill and malformed at his evil glance and were outcast from Enchanted City. These were the lucky ones. Others went away forever into a country that was only in their minds.

Carny lived in a huge mansion on the edge of the mountain that rose behind Enchanted City. Mt. Hill lifted its grand peak to the sky and proudly displayed a vast array of large estates and palatial homes. The child's father was a wealthy merchant who traveled far to purchase costly goods for sale in the city bazaar.

Carny had everything a girl could want. She never went hungry or shivered in the cold. Her father was rich enough to hire servants. Her mother was beautiful and kind. She had no brothers or sisters demanding to share her toys.

But something was wrong. Something was so wrong with Carny that her mother wept quietly in the day when everyone else was sleeping. Her father walked around with a worried frown creasing a deep line between his eyes. The servants huddled in groups discussing the girl's sorry condition.

Carny stayed in her room. She refused to look out her windows at the lovely, starry nights. The shutters were locked, the blinds were shut, and the heavy winter tapestries were always drawn. The only persons allowed in the room were Nurse (who left carrying silver trays of half-eaten food) and Carny's mother (who stayed only for short visits)—but never her father. He, unfortunately, reminded his daughter of the Enchanter.

All the old-time servants remembered that the girl had once been a happy, beautiful little pixie with sparkling brown eyes and lustrous, curly black hair. Her cheeks dimpled when she smiled—and she was always smiling, dancing about, full of embraces for everyone.

"She was a luv," they'd whisper to one another, their starched headpieces bobbing in the tight circle. "Such a luv. So sad."

But five terrible years ago it had happened. The Enchanter's Ball, held yearly at a mansion of the wizard's own choosing, took place that year at the marble and cedar palace of Carny's father. The house had been filled with fire priests, and the evil Enchanter's minions stood guard around all the revelers who laughed and danced and *acted* as though they were having a good time—although some admitted it was hard to have fun on command.

That night Carny had been safely tucked in bed. Mothers hid their children out of sight when the Enchanter was nearby—not because the Enchanter didn't like children, no, no. The problem was he liked them too much and in all the wrong ways. Orphans, of course, belonged to the Enchanter; they became his forced labor to do the dirty work of Enchanted City. But children of the wealthy were not beyond his conscription. Many a beautiful child had been drafted to serve as a pampered attendant in the Dagoda. Few parents considered this a privilege.

Downstairs the music played. Bells sewn to the hems of fire priests' robes jangled. Laughter and merriment called the little child from her deep sleep. She crept from bed and tiptoed to the circular railing that guarded the bedroom corridor from the vast space that arched to the great ceiling above and to the grand ballroom below. She would find her mother, she thought. Thumb in her mouth, dressed in snug pajamas, she descended the stairs, step by step, her hand gripping the bannister.

No one noticed her—not the laughing adults, not the servants hurrying by with trays of drinks and apertifs—but her little eyes caught sight of the tallest man in the hall. She stopped, one foot in midair, and stared. He was wearing the most beautiful robe; it flashed as he turned and shimmered as he swayed. His amber hair was brilliant and soft. It was the Enchanter, at his most attractive, in rare party form.

Suddenly, he turned where he was standing as though he felt her eyes on him. The man fixed his look on her, capturing her eyes with his own. It was too late too look away, too late, too late. She was a beautiful child. He waved his hands in the air, casting an enchantment; sparks flew from his fingertips. And though the music played on, everyone in the room stood stone still. The man left the party and walked across the room to the grand staircase and the child. He climbed each step slowly, one at a time, his gaze burning with intensity.

Mesmerized as she was, child though she was, she sensed danger. She backed up a stair, her thumb still in her mouth. His look was hot, and she was afraid. He looked at her a long time, and she felt his stare pierce to her very soul. "*Mama!*" she finally cried.

And the spell was broken. People finished the laugh that had been interrupted and the thought in mid-sentence and the incomplete dance step. Though the music played and the room was suddenly filled with merriment again, her beautiful mother came running, her long silken dress rustling.

She lifted her daughter in her arms. "What are you doing out of bed?"

The Enchanter spoke, "You have a very lovely child there."

Carny could feel her mother shiver.

Carny was taken back to her room and tucked into her feather-quilted bed, but when she woke in the morning she couldn't bear for anyone to look at her or to look into her eyes.

So the curtains were drawn, because she was afraid someone was peering in at her. And the doctors her father called frightened her more, and when they looked at her, she slipped far away from them, far away through a small door to a place where she could hide and where no one could find her.

She slipped onto a roller coaster car and rode it swooping up and down, away from the eyes, the eyes. Up, far, far up, slowly, slowly; then a rush, then a running ride, then a wooshing down, down, down. Into carnival land she went.

And when her mother came, calling her name, "*Carny!*" she had gone far, far away. Into the tilting boxes of the Ferris wheel. Up and around and high, staying high at the apex; slower, then faster, then faster, then slower. Looking down she could see her mother, her beautiful mother, far down. She could see her mother's tears swell and drop, becoming frozen crystals which grew to large

cubes of ice, catching shafts of light, shards of hard brilliance, sparkling, glittering, then exploding in fireworks—BLA-CHEW-AH! BLA-CHEW-AH!

Nurse always crept quietly in the shadows of the hushed closed room, casting down her eyes. She held the girl until the carnival music had quieted, and the vendors had stopped calling, "This-away! This-away! Getcher ticket he-ah!" Nurse held her until the carnival girl had stopped hiding in the noisy clamor that was her own mind.

Her father came once, and his look of concern sent the child farther into carnival land than she had ever been. He paced outside her door, and the servants whispered and held their starched aprons to their faces. They could all hear the child screaming in terror as she swooped high on the roller coaster and then rushed down, only to climb slowly up again and again.

The Ferris wheel going round and round. The roller coaster going up and down, down and around. The carousel going around and around. The organ music grinding, "Boom! pa-da! Boom! pa-da! Boom! pa-da-DA!"

Everyone missed the lovely little girl who had danced and laughed and loved. Everyone was glad when she had quiet days and seemed more like her old self. And everyone dreaded the moments when a thoughtless look or even an imagined glance would send the child on the carnival rides that went on and on and never closed down and never moved to the next town.

"Don't look—don't look at me-e-e-e-e!" Carny would scream when no one was even in her room and when all the drapes were tightly closed. And when Nurse would rush to check, she knew by the faraway look on the child's face that the music had begun again and that from the distant height of the inward Ferris wheel, she herself was only a tiny speck on the ground and her own cry, "Come back! Don't go away!" could scarcely be heard.

For five years Carny went away in her mind, afraid that *he* would come and sear her again with a glance. Any looks of love or only of casual interest, reminded her of that night when he had captured her with his burning eyes. "Don't look! Don't look!" she would cry and go away.

Each time she returned, she was thinner, more worn, as though the journey was too difficult for a child to make by herself. All who loved her suffered, but most of all her father who mourned deeply his exile from his own daughter in his own house.

One midday she was wakened by her mother's whisper, *"Can you help her?"* Carny kept her eyes closed. Not another doctor. They were all Enchanter's men who sent her far away. If she just didn't look. If she just wouldn't remember.

A man's voice answered quietly, "Yes, I can help her."

Not another, she thought. Fear knotted its fist in her chest. She moaned and began scrambling toward the keyhole entrance in her mind to escape.

She's awake, said her mother. *She's going. Carny, don't go. Don't go. Someone is here who can help you.*

In a hurry, Carny found the little door that opened from here to there. But before she slipped through, she heard the man say, "Don't worry. I'll go with her."

Then the carnival music hid the sounds. Carnival fireworks exploded— BLA-CHEW-AH! BLA-CHEW-AH! Carney barkers shouted, "Pee-nuts! Pop-corn! Cotton-can-dee!"

The merry-go-round, thought Carny. *No one can find me. The merry-go-round goes round and round, and the painted horses go up and down. I can run and hide and stay there forever and ever.*

BLA-CHEW-AH! Round and up and round and down. Pee-nuts! Popcorn! Getcher ticket he-ah! Round and up and round and down. BLA-CHEW-AH!

The farther she rode, the more Carny thought she heard someone calling her name. She rode and rode on the painted pony until she was out of breath.

It was a man's voice! If she could only drown it in the carnival music. "Boom! pa-da! Boom! pa-da! Boom! pa-da-DA!"

But she still heard him calling, "Carny! Carny!"

The Enchanter! She knew what his evil eye had spoken when she was just a little girl still sucking her thumb and cuddled in warm pajamas: *"You are mine. All mine."* She had always known that one day when she was grown, the fire wizard would come to get her. With one look he would capture her eyes, and she would be helpless but to follow.

This time she would stay here in carnival land and ride the carousel round and round and up and down forever and forever.

"Carny! Carny!"

With a sigh, Carny gave up. She dismounted the painted pony she had been riding. It was no use. He was here, the Enchanter. She might as well look into his hot eyes. How could she resist one who could follow her through the secret keyhole, into this Boom! pa-da! madness, round and up and round and down.

With a sob, the girl looked toward the place from where his call had come. Yes, a man was standing in the middle of the carousel, under the arch of the turning roof. She could go round and round forever but he would always be in the center of her turning.

"Carny!" he called again. "Don't be afraid!"

Carny lifted her eyes to see—not the Enchanter, but a most beautiful young man. She cast her eyes quickly down again.

"Carny, look up!"

Something in the young man's tone banished her fear. She lifted her eyes, and for the first time in years looked full into a face. The wound within which had ached and throbbed with pain began to ease.

He reached his hand to her—and in a moment, in wonder, she lifted hers across the painted ponies to him. At his touch the merry-go-round music began to slow, the blasting of the fireworks began to stop, the carnival music grew silent: *"Boom-pa-da . . . pa . . . da . . . p.a.a.a.a.a.a.a.a. . . ."*

She was in her room when she came to herself, with her mother's shocked face close. Nurse suddenly drew the draperies open, lifted the blinds, threw apart the shutters. Light, glorious light, flooded the once dark place.

She was still in her bed. The eiderdown was rumpled and moist with sweat. She was still holding the young man's hand. She was still looking into his eyes. But he was smiling the gentlest of smiles, and his look was full of a love that could capture you—but only if you wanted it to.

"Oh, Mother," she sighed. "I have been so far away."

Her mother was crying now, but her tears were ordinary tears that glistened on her cheeks and fell on the pillow where Carny's head rested.

Then she remembered. It had been years. "Where is my father?" she asked. "It's been so long since I've seen my father."

Carny's mother looked up at the young man, questioning. He nodded his head, and Nurse rushed from the room to wake Carny's father from his fitful sleep.

"How can we ever thank you?" said Carny's mother. Carny thought she was so beautiful with her eyes moist and shining.

The young man smiled again, bent, and kissed the palm of Carny's hand, which he then placed beneath the coverlet. "Become a part of the resistance that is working for the restoration of my kingdom," he answered. "Throw all your resources into it. But only if you think it's a cause worth living and dying for."

At that moment Carny's father rushed into the room. He knelt by her bed and looked into her eyes, and the two of them embraced each other and wept aloud. Through her tears, she could see the young man shaking her mother's hand and accepting Nurse's grateful hug. Then the man moved through the doorway where the bevy of sleepy but curious servants were crowding and peering into her room.

Don't go away, she thought. *I want to look into your eyes one more time.*

But she remained silent, because she knew that One who could enter into the middle of madness in order to lead her safely out would always be at the center of her life, no matter how far she journeyed. She knew she would never again be out of the loving circle of his gaze.

The Orphan Exodus

The Dagoda: a palace of brooding towers and iron gates, of council chambers to devise unjust deeds and of courtrooms to sentence the innocent, of fire priests' cells and the secret service garrison, of prison and torture chambers, of the orphan pavilion where frightened orphans are drilled under the cruel hand of the Orphan Keeper. From this evil center the Enchanter casts his dark spells.

The King and Big Operator approached the Dagoda. Burners guarded all entrances, their pokers glowling luridly in the dark while squads of Breakers boot-stomped in and out, cudgels held attack-ready. Both men knew it was a dangerous night.

The King whispered, "The Enchanter is readying his forces for assault. Our time is very short." Big Operator nodded. They must do what they had come to do quickly lest their bold plan be aborted.

For days the drivers and dispatchers had watched the King and the chief huddled together behind the glassed-in office of the City Taxi Company— another rescue strategy was in the making. All sensed the bond of love between the two as they concentrated on unfolded maps on the desk, but none knew the plan they were devising was so desperate it could well be Big Operator's last.

Shortly, vanguard orders for an orphan exodus appeared at the dispatcher control panel. The next night the fleet of swift taxis crept with dimmed headlights through the streets, disconnected from the power source, and took to back alleys. They were to surround the Enchanter's Dagoda, await the signal, and then whisk as many escapees from the orphan pavilion as possible to the edge of the garbage dump, where the King himself would accompany the children to Great Park.

The orphan pavilion was to one side of the Dagoda, enclosed by a high wall with a surrounding courtyard. A sign beside the tall gate proclaimed "WE LOVE CHILDREN—Orphan Keepers' Association," but everyone in Enchanted City knew that children were loved only because they provided forced labor to do the dirty work of the Enchanter.

Two huge wolves the size of lions guarded either side of the entrance. They growled as the men approached; they bared their teeth and drooled. A soft light gathered around the King. The wolves stared, whimpered, and then hid their heads in their paws while the two men passed them by. All closed places opened to the King when he so willed it.

Inside, a squad of orphans wearing tattered rags scrubbed the courtyard. A keeper's assistant with a whistle around her neck chanted, "Clean-clean-clean!" and stood ready to beat the slow workers with a long stick. Another work detail, a long line of children tied together at the ankles with rough sections of rope, were getting ready to collect the city garbage which citizens tossed on the street. A whistle blew—*Hweet! Hweet!*—and the crew marched to the waiting carts while another assistant prodded them with the sharp tines of her forked shovel.

Huge vats of water boiled while children stirred the dirty clothes within. The hot water splashed on the orphans' rags, burning them one moment and then soaking them to the skin in the cold night. An assistant prodded them with a long wooden turning spoon. *Hweet!* she blew her whistle and shouted, "Scroundrels! Dimwits! I'll boil *you* if you spill any more wash water!" *Hweet!*

All the orphans, boys and girls, wore the same haircuts, making it nearly impossible to tell one from another. Their clothes were an identical gray which grew increasingly threadbare during washings as they were passed down from one child to another. Skinny, sad eyed, covered with sores from the lack of proper foods, not one orphan smiled or laughed or told jokes or chased another in games of tag. Games were forbidden, and play had been outlawed. No one belonged to any other—brothers and sisters were separated. There were no holidays and never any birthday cakes.

Lanterns cast a dim light in the dark courtyard. Big Operator and the King could see another work detail carrying brooms, preparing to march out to sweep the streets. The workers were all barefoot, and the night was cold.

"Hey-ya!" shouted their assistant keeper, and bleated on her whistle *Hweet! Hweet! Hweet!* As one, the troop centered the broom handles on their shoulders. "I told ya t'keep t'line!" shouted the guard again, and she stomped on the foot of a little child who had stumbled. "Got'cher!" shouted the keeper cruelly as the child dropped the broom and grasped the poor foot but uttered not a sound. The penalty for sobbing was a hot poker prod.

Big Operator seethed with enormous rage. It was against this abuse that he had given his life, against this outrage that he had masterminded the resistance, against these indignities that he had worked for the Restoration. He wanted to yell and shout; he wanted to take that guard and shake her by her shoulders. The King restrained him with his hand. Then a voice demanded, "What you going in here? No outsiders allowed on the premises!"

It was an older child dressed in faded blue—an orphan who had come up through orphan ranks and was now dressed in the uniform of an assistant in training. He was still barefoot; only full-fledged assistants were issued footwear. Their food rations were also increased from one meal a day to two, and they were given whistles. For some that was reason enough to mistreat one's fellow orphan.

"Hello, Jason," said the King. "We've come to speak to the Orphan Keeper."

At the sound of his name, the boy's eyes widened. Orphans were addressed only by number and rank; the last person who had spoken his name had been his mother, years ago, so long ago he could scarcely remember her face or the sound of her voice. The boy cocked his head as though listening to something far away, something almost forgotten. He moved closer. "Who-who are you?" he whispered, his voice very low.

The King answered in the same way, gently, careful not to frighten the orphan. "I am the King."

"How—how did you know my name?"

"I know all the names of the ones who belong to me."

At that moment a siren horn blared, whistles blew—*Hweet! Hweet!*—and all the orphans closed ranks hup-to! hup-to! hup-to! and stood at attention. The assistant orphan keepers saluted in front of their squads. All was quiet in the courtyard, except for the sound of orphans' snuffling runny noses and the stamp-stamp-stamp of frozen feet on cold hard stones and the wailing of the night wind out of Enchanted City.

"She comes," whispered the child. "She comes each night for inspection." The expression in his eyes looked as though a brief glimpse into a world once loved and longed for had been shattered. In terror, the boy ran to find his place.

Suddenly, a woman appeared at the inside entrance to the orphans' pavilion. She was tall and beautiful and wore glamorous clothes—purple fitted pants with matching purple boots and a flowing red robe which she swept from one side to another behind her. She cracked a cat-o'-nine-tails in her hand. A golden headdress embossed with flames crowned her brilliant black hair. She wore bracelets and rings and ear loops and one glittering necklace draped over another and another. Drummers rolled the announcement of her appearing—*tatatatatatatatatatatatatatatataTA-TA!*

Beside her stood two Burners with glowing pokers. Keeper assistants bowed in the ranks, their whistles clattering on the paving stones. Torchbearers lit her path. With each step the Orphan Keeper's jewels glimmered and glistened in the reflected torchlight. Her severe beauty was chiseled by the hard edge of hatred; her eyes flashed with malignant power over the orphans who had been entrusted to her keeping. There was nothing soft in all her body or in all her soul.

"I am the Orphan Keeper," she intoned. "You will do my bidding. You will keep my commands. I have control over your lives and your destinies. I am the one who says yea and nay. You can never escape. You can never go where I say no."

The children cowered, even the older ones. All knew this loveless woman had power to send them to the underworld, to poison their food and call it nightailment, to advance them or to cut off their rations. It was she who ordered punishment for all if one orphan misbehaved.

"You are mine! You are all mine!" she shouted again, lashing the air with the hand whip.

"LET MY CHILDREN GO!"

Everyone within the courtyard froze. The drums stopped in mid-roll *tatatata—TA?* Who dared disrupt the Orphan Keeper's time schedule? Who dared interrupt her early night-work-duty harangue? The children shivered in the cold, miserable with hunger and now with dread. What torture would they suffer because of this unspeakable challenge?

The King had shouted the words. He faced the Orphan Keeper,

throwing the hood of his common garment back from his head as though she would recognize him once his face was fully revealed in the torchlight. The children gasped at such defiance. Who was this man?

The King's hair glimmered with gold highlights and his loosened street robe fell to the paving stones and he stood strong and tall and broad shouldered and handsome. Big Operator gasped—he had never beheld his King undisguised, so young and so beautiful.

The Orphan Keeper cracked her cat-o'-nine-tails in the air. "I know you, you troublemaker. You instigator! Who do you think you are, challenging my power? The Enchanter has cast his spell over these children. They are mine! I can do what I please with them."

The King answered her not a word, but all could see he was as angry as she. He crossed the pavement and lifted his hands. A wind began to blow, around and around, *who-hooooo-ooo; who-hooooo-ooo*. It caught the torches of the torchbearers and bound the flames in one windy firebrand—*who-hooooo-ooo: who-hooooo-ooo!* Up—up!—it shot into the night sky over the orphan pavilion, blazing. By its light all could see the King grab the hand whip from the Orphan Keeper's grasp, lash the pokers from the Burner's hands, scatter the assistants with a crack, and then toss the instruments of torture to the sky. A bolt of lightning flashed from nowhere, striking with a CRA—A—A—CK! Flames burst and a ball of fire fell to the ground, finally to be extinguished at the Orphan Keeper's feet.

The ranks of orphans gasped. The assistant keepers hid their prodding spoons, sticks, and shovels behind their backs, dropped them to the ground, or pushed them under carts.

Then in the unlit dark all could see the warm radiance of the man standing in the middle of the courtyard, daring to defy the evil power of the Orphan Keeper herself. The King signaled to Big Operator and together, with a mighty thrust, they overturned the boiling vat of palace laundry. They ripped the wheels from the work carts, their muscles straining in a fury of indignation.

And no one moved to stop them. The Burners stood mesmerized. No warning signal was given to the Dagoda. The Orphan Keeper hissed as though air was escaping from her lungs—*s-s-s-s-s-s-s*.

Many of the children dropped to their knees, clasping their hands together beneath their chins, scarcely daring to hope. Was this one who could save them? Would their misery finally end? Was freedom close?

The King straightened himself again and stared the Orphan Keeper in the eyes. "You mistake yourself, madame," he said. His voice was tight with controlled wrath. "These children are not yours; they belong to me."

With those words he motioned to Big Operator, who stepped forward, wiping axle grease from his hands on his overalls. He bent his knee and bowed. Though comrade to the King before, he was an obedient subject now.

"Is the taxi vanguard ready?" asked the King.

"Yes, my Lord. Ready and waiting." His voice was full of satisfaction.

At that the Orphan Keeper screamed, staggering on her feet. "S-s-s-s. You!—you! You can't take thes-s-s-e children! They're waifs-s-s-s-s! They're cavils-s-s-s, slaves-s-s-s-s! The wolves-s-s-s-s will tear them to shreds-s-s-s-s.

They do my bidding! They won't come with you! S-s-s-s."

Paying no attention, the King lifted his crossed arms and spread them in a circle above his head. More light diffused from his stretching embrace, till it filled every corner of the grim courtyard. The orphans' frozen feet began to warm; their cold, wet garments began to dry; their wounds and sores began to heal in the gentle light. Their hearts began to mend.

"What you don't understand, madame," said the King, "is that every orphan answers when his name is called in love."

Then the King began to call their names, names unspoken for months, for years, names they themselves had almost forgotten. He called them in family groups, brothers and sisters, brothers and brothers, sisters and sisters, according to age and position. He spoke their names with tenderness, with kindly affection, with cherished intimacy as though he had been practicing them for years.

"Kristen, Ned, James, Sara, and Susan.

Anne, Ted, John, and Linda.

Jason and Maria.

Alex, Sharon, and Rob.

Eric, Jane, and Cathy.

Diane . . ."

And each child remembered his or her name. And each child stepped from the ranks. He was more than a number, more than flesh for the meat grinder of the Enchanter's labor machines. He had a name chosen in love and a family history and a King who was worthy of service.

Big Operator stood now at the street entrance to the pavilion; the beastly wolves lay silent in a stupor of sleep. He put two fingers to his mouth and blew a cabbie signal. At this, his master strategy went into operation. The first taxi accelerated to curbside, the first ready orphan group climbed into the back and front seats. The driver honked and then hurried off toward the garbage dump as another cab pulled up to take another load, followed by another and another.

And inside the King continued to speak the children's names, and with each naming the Orphan Keeper grew grayer, more haggard, leaking hot air. Her hair lost its luster, her teeth grew black and straggly until all could see her for her true self: a wicked hag who had gorged on the energy and youth and beauty of the children given to her keeping, a faker whose evil power was not her own, a no-people in disguise, as were all who gave themselves to do the will of the Enchanter. Finally she was nothing but a pile of dust covered by filthy red and purple rags, her gold melted and her jewels turned to powder.

And Big Operator was glad; his heart leaped with gladness. He knew the Enchanter would take revenge, but if this be his last strategic rescue design ever, he had been at the side of his King as together they emptied the pavilion of every last orphan. He closed his eyes and listened to the taxi vanguard, *his* taxi vanguard, honking throughout all of Enchanted City. HARNK! HARNK!—here, there, and everywhere—HARNK! HARNK! It sounded in his ears like a raucous chorus of jubilant rescue.

The King stood beside him ready to leave and to accompany the escapees into Great Park. The handclasp between them was firm and long. Their anger was gone but, strangely, there was no exultation, just a quiet sadness. Both knew what dire consequences their defiant acts would set into motion. "Farewell," said the King, and they embraced, the embrace of two mighty men. The orphan exodus was accomplished.

Big Operator watched the King disappear into the night. And though he knew it was just his imagination, it seemed as though a crowd of children stood all over the city, clapping their hands and shouting "Bravo!" And when the last taxi had hurried away with the last load, on a whim Big Operator bowed to the city—and the applause rose louder in his heart.

For Big Operator had learned through the years of masterminding the taxi resistance that mighty deeds demand mighty risks, but that it is worth risking all for the sake of the Kingdom and the King.

The Enchanter's Revenge

The fiery rage of the Enchanter flamed.
Revenge for the orphan exodus fell wrathfully on the City Taxi
Company, and after Burners and Breakers had conducted a brutal
demolition raid on the terminal, the evil eye of the Enchanter
hunted for one victim more.

The warning bell in the underground garage was still clamoring. Barely moments had passed since the merciless attack had come and gone. Cabbies and mechanics stumbled to their feet, shaken by the brutal hostilities of the cudgels and burning pokers of the raiding secret police. Torn from the wall, the map of Enchanted City burned on the floor. The control panel had been ruthlessly smashed as well as the glassed-in operations office. Fires blazed in overturned buckets of greasy rags and licked their hungry tongues toward nearby oil and grease slicks.

Hero climbed through a ragged hole in the overhead door, which now hung askew, and entered the garage. He had gone to the garbage dump to see if there was any sight of a returning king. Acrid smoke from the oil fires choked him,

and with one quick look he surveyed the devastation. The Enchanter had had his revenge. Paint had been dashed against the fleet of taxis. Windshields had been smashed, doors and fenders bludgeoned. Half-opened hoods showed wires and cords ripped from the motor bellies of engines.

He motioned to several cabbies, and together they struggled to slide the huge gaping door from its rollers so fresh air could blow into the smoky underground.

The siren of the warning bell wailed uselessly. Hero looked at the dismembered control panel—no more rescue operations would be dispatched here! The resistance had been effectively disabled. But now, to the fires! to the wounded! A moment of panic—Amanda! Where was that girl? Then out of the corner of his eye, he saw her tearing bandages, wiping away soot and blood from the head of a cabby, her own face darkened by smoke and streaked with tears.

"This ain't the worst of it!" shouted Mac the Mechanic, hurrying past with buckets of sawdust to smother the flames of oil fires. She tossed him a shovel. "Took Big Operator. Roughed him up bad. Dragged him outta here. Weren't nothin' we could do to stop 'em."

Hero groaned as he spaded sawdust and sand. Big Operator was the brains of the Resistance. He had masterminded hundreds of daring rescues, and in such clever ways, that until very recently, all strategy had struck at the strength of the Enchanter without incurring his wrath. But there was no time now for worry. They had all they could do to salvage something from the wreck of the City Taxi Company.

The days that followed were wearying, worrisome. All hands worked on the dismembered fleet of taxis. Mechanics attempted to reconstruct engines, the worst fire damage was repaired, everyone learned to live with the lingering bitter smell of smoke. Charred cars and equipment (as well as the smashed control panel) were junked. Wounds and bruises began to heal. But no cabbies dared to take the few remaining taxis out into the streets. The evil of enchantment hung heavy on their heads; no one would venture to guess whether or when the Enchanter would strike again.

Besides, their hearts were heavy; defeat hung in the bitter air; there was no room for jaunty resistance. No word had come of Big Operator.

And what was the resistance without Big Operator? The taxi vanguard was his strategy; the central dispatcher system, the safe-houses scattered across the city for orphan and outcast refuge, the storage cell power sources, the methods of sighting—all these were his ideas.

With the map destroyed, it became even more important for Hero to keep an accurate Chronicle of Sightings, so that none of this time would be lost to memory. After working exhausting hours each night with the cleanup crews, he spent weary days writing down details, remembering himself or interviewing those who remembered, the hows, whens, and wherefores of Sightings of the King.

He worked at the desk behind the broken glass panels of Big Operator's office. Naysaying choked his spirit. The Resistance was shattered. There had been no Sightings of the King since the orphan exodus. No one could break the Enchanter's spell. And if the King returned?—what could anyone do even then?

Sitting at Big Operator's desk, he kept thinking of all the chief had taught him since he returned from Great Park. With their common city background, they understood one another; the gruff older man had been like a father to Hero, the father he had never known, a patient teacher.

The second night, Amanda came to sit beside him. "Can I help?" she asked. With emergency nursing behind her and dispatcher responsibilities ended, she had time on her hands.

Hero sighed. The Chronicle was almost current. The orphan exodus had been recorded and he had only to write about these recent terrible events. "I think I can remember everything Big Operator ever said to me." He leaned back in the chair and quoted the chief. " 'This is an occupied city; we are in the midst of enemy territory.'

"He was a rough man, Amanda,—but, everyone in the City Taxi Company knew he was a man of the mind as well. It was the chief who collected the fragments of song and unwritten stories from the tale keepers for the Chronicle. Without them that history would be almost forgotten—the tales of the always young King who once ruled this city with a firm but benevolent hand, of the Age of Rebellion when the Enchanter lured away the loyalty of the citizenry, of how the King went into exile vowing to return when time enough had passed for all to discover the folly of such a choice, and of how the fire wizard placed an enchantment over the city and ruled his subjects with the power of fire."

Hero paused, remembering. "My own mother must have been a tale keeper—keeping alive the old, true tales. I remember her words on her dying bed: 'There is a King, a real King!' "

Amanda felt tired and saddened. When would they ever be able to go back to the old ways of field and forest?

"You love him, don't you?" she said, smiling gently.

"Yes," said Hero. "He's a gruff old gizzard, but he's a genius, too. He'd been experimenting with daylight. 'The whole city's supposed to run on it!' he'd say. Solar panels. Storage cells. Sun batteries. He was getting us ready to live in the Restoration, to live at day and sleep at night, to harness the sun to do the work that slave labor does now."

Amanda quoted Big Operator: "Work in harmony with the world; not in disharmony with it!" She punched the air with her fist. This was a favorite City Taxi Company saying; they almost heard his rough voice again. The two smiled sadly at each other.

With that Hero leaned his elbows forward on the desk and hid his face in his hands. His voice was tight with grief. "He's dead, Amanda. I know it in my heart. I can only hope that he died quickly."

The two were silent. Amanda didn't protest, didn't work to evoke false hope. She had already seen this terrible truth deep in her own heart. After a while she spoke, "Did anyone tell you what Big Operator's last words were when he was taken captive? You'll need it for the Chronicle."

Hero shook his bowed head, and she continued. "He had been badly beaten; three or four Breakers attacked him. Destruction was dismantling his lifework; but as they were dragging him away, he struggled to his feet and called out for all of us to hear above the din, 'The Restoration is near!' They knocked him senseless as he must have known they would. But, Hero, I keep hearing his cry, over and over—*The Restoration is near!*"

Hero tilted up his head, still braced in the cup of his hands, and looked at Amanda. She always had perfect aim. That and her gift of seeing had made her the quickest dispatcher in the Resistance. The girl leaned over and compassionately touched his face. Did she realize she had covered his scar with her hand? He didn't think she had even noticed. She had certainly comforted the scar in his heart.

All that day, with sidelong glances, Hero watched Amanda. She was not the same as she had been. Hero missed her old impudence, the riotous imagination, the derring-do that went to combat with any opponent no matter how huge. When she laughed, most infrequently now, he was flooded with memories of sunlight and a burning circle of flames. He missed his old play friend.

He reminded himself that though she had never gone through branding she had once been badly burned—evil fire of any kind always wounds the one it touches. Now, she was an alien in an enemy camp, a princess in disguise, and he suspected, though she never spoke of it nor complained of her assignment in this dreadful place, that she longed each moment for the beauty and sanctuary of Great Park.

And yet in some ways, she was the same. She was still spirited. It was a determined Amanda who had rescued the Forbidden Princess, who despite the risk to herself had undertaken the dangerous work of naming the Names on the very street of the Dagoda. Sitting in that rescue taxi, flooded with relief that his friend was safe with the King—that had been the first time he had noticed how tall she had grown and that her freckles were gone.

She was changed—but then, they were all changed. She reminded him of someone—someone he knew well and couldn't place. He watched during those days of recovery as she read portions of the Chronicle to those who were still mending from injuries, as she cheerfully carried iron pots of hot broth at mealtimes, as she tenderly calmed anxiety among the rough drivers who chafed at the waiting and disablement. Now and then she told funny little stories, and his heart gladdened at her laughter.

She was still spirited, but in a subdued sort of way. And every once in a while she flared; her eyes flashed; she became indignant. She reminded him of the embers that fly when cooling coals are stirred. She was like—like Mercie! Amanda reminded him of Mercie.

Despite himself, as he carefully finished the Chronicle, helped to reorganize the taxi crew, waited impatiently for a word about Big Operator or

a Sighting of the King, Hero realized that he cared deeply for his onetime play friend. And he knew she could never care for him in the same way. She was of the fields; he could still see it in her eyes—the meadows, the birdsong, the dappled light. He was of these city streets, dark and devastating. He knew its ways, was at home in its dead-ends and confusion. Amanda felt ill at ease here and always would.

Furthermore, Amanda was a princess of the royal line. He had seen her at becoming, when she became real, a dazzlingly beautiful child. Her Taxi Company overalls were only a disguise. It was he who was the former orphan, a street waif, a refugee who had barely escaped the Enchanter's designs, upon whom the merciful people of Great Park had taken pity.

And though these days he rarely thought about the scar, he knew his face was so disfigured no young woman could ever want him. Besides, this was an inopportune place for love, this dangerous time, this evil moment locked in desperate confrontation with the diabolical.

So Hero was silent and waited for his disturbing feelings to pass.

Then one lonely outpost sentry returned, banging on the bent and broken metal of the overhead door which had been patched. A mechanic cranked it open and closed again. A report of a Sighting! Street people talked of a group who had come from the place where trees grew, through the old gates, across the garbage dump.

And the next night, the King himself returned to the dispirited City Taxi Company. It was he who brought the word which they all had been dreading: Big Operator was dead.

They mourned at what they had all feared. Each reached a hand to the next. They put arms around each other, seeking comfort. The jaunty resistance was no more.

And the King walked among them, as grieved as they. Big Operator and he had loved each other. And he whispered to each, "The Restoration is at hand. . . ."

Despite their tears, all remembered that these words had been Big Operator's last.

"Don't be discouraged," he said. "The time of resistance is almost past."

He gathered his faithful subjects into the great cavern of the underground terminal, those Rangers who had bravely infiltrated Enchanted City, the mechanics and drivers and duty persons of the taxi resistance. "Soon," the King said, "the Enchantment over the city will be lifted. But you must be brave. You must not lose heart. The spell of the evil fire wizard can only be broken by the act of a willing victim."

His words were terrible to them, though they didn't understand what he meant. Each looked into his or her own heart to examine the degree of willingness, and they were afraid.

Then the King held out one hand to Amanda and the other to Hero and to all those who had learned the music of Great Park. A meager band of Rangers wearing Taxi Company overalls formed a sentry circle. And there the King began the Great Celebration. Cabbies took overturned oil drums and beat out the rhythm that they heard, and the sound echoed in the hollow of the terminal. Others clapped time with their hands—a soft beat, filled with mourning.

There was no splendor of vaulted forest above, no gifted entertainment, no lavish banquet spread before them. There was no leaping grandeur of the Circle of Sacred Flames. The rhythm was somber, slow moving, and sad—but it was the Great Celebration just the same.

And those from Great Park who knew and remembered the ancient steps joined hands and made entrance in their hearts and became real. And as they passed each other, turning in the well-known patterns, music rose in their souls and peace came to their minds even while the intense darkness outside gathered for a final onslaught. Then it was that Amanda looked into Hero's eyes and saw with her deep sight what he couldn't and wouldn't speak. She saw that he loved her.

For love is a gift that surprises us even in the despairing moments of danger or death, and by this we know it mirrors a greater love, one which is never ending.

Traffic Court

Traffic Court was in the very middle of the hold of the Dagoda. Here the people of the city were tried for minor and major traffic offenses—crossing streets at night during a power out, impeding the progress of the Enchanter's limousines, failing to yield to emergency vehicles, walking instead of riding when the man-made power was working. But the charge made no difference in this courtroom of the Enchanter. No one was ever declared innocent.

Amanda stood trembling in a darkened corner of Traffic Court. She couldn't help herself; she had never felt the tremendous power of evil so forcefully. She had to labor to catch a breath, as though in this stronghold of the fire wizard, air smothered her lungs. The evil power made her shoulders ache; it pressed against the backs of her eyes, pushed hard against her stomach. She needed all the strength she could muster to withstand its insistent oppression.

The King had been captured the night before, after leading the sad and sorrowful Great Celebration. He had been charged with a felony, organizing the taxi resistance; with high treason in proclaiming another kingdom; with heinous insurrection—pretending to be the King! All charges bore the penalty of death by burning at Burning Place.

Amanda drew another deep breath, struggling to fill her lungs. Around the courtroom, iron braziers held burning coals which emitted a red and eerie glow. The benches began to fill with street people. The Chief Herald of the Enchanter shuffled papers on the judge's dais; he tested his proclamation horn.

Surviving members of the underground taxi resistance had decided it was unwise for the Keeper of the Chronicle of the Sightings of the King to attend this trial. Hero had attracted the attention of the Enchanter's eye all too often, his scar, as well as his tendency to take bold action, made him conspicuous. So Amanda, with her quiet gifts of seeing and aiming, was chosen to walk alone through the gates of the Enchanter's palace and simply to observe the proceedings. She was pledged to take no action on the King's behalf—it would be foolish. Most felt he was a dead man already; there was no use risking two lives, and maybe all the lives of those in the Resistance, if she should behave unwisely.

The courtroom was now full. The Clerk of Traffic Court entered and banged the gavel; sparks flew as though iron and flint had been struck. "All rise!" he cried. "Hear ye! Hear ye! The Traffic Court of the Enchanter in the Keep of the Grand Dagoda is now in session!"

All the street people, family members and friends of the accused, struggled to their feet, the great weight of dark oppression crushing their shoulders. They all knew the traffic charge made no difference. Whether they had committed major or minor offenses or were wrongfully accused, they paid exorbitant fines. They forfeited lands and goods; they were condemned to hard labor; they were proclaimed unworthy parents and had their children sentenced to the Orphan Keeper. All were judged guilty.

The Chief Herald blew his horn and the song of the Naysayers began. Marching feet signaled the presence of the guard of Burners and Breakers—soon these surrounded the edge of the courtroom. The death drums sounded—*din-din-din-din*. Then suddenly, the room was filled with a fiery light as the Enchanter himself made his entrance to be the judge of tonight's trials.

Amanda felt despair, whiplike, lash itself around her heart. She had never known evil so real. It breathed; it sang terrible melodies; it dug fangs into her spirit and injected her with a venom—poisonous, rank, life threatening.

The Enchanter's cloak was like warm fire on the hearth. It glowed and curled, inviting and mesmerizing. But his eyes, his eyes were malevolent, filled with yellow light and gleeful, exultant, triumphant.

The prisoners, doleful and miserable, were brought to the dock. Guards

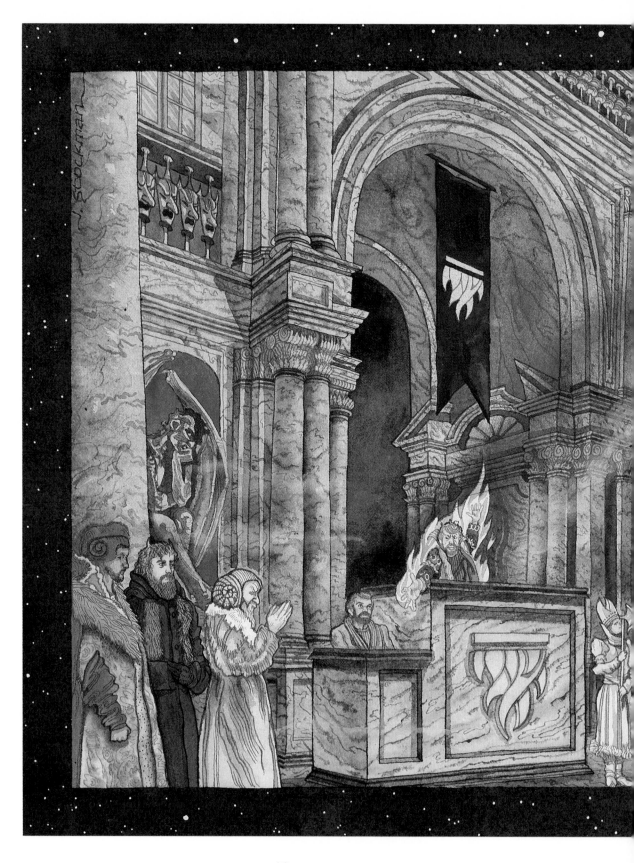

handled them roughly, pushing and shoving them into place.

Amanda leaned closer: *Which is the King?* She couldn't find him. Had he been tortured, like Big Operator, without sentencing?'

"Quiet in the courtroom," announced the Clerk, striking his iron gavel on its flint pad. The Enchanter had slipped into the black robes of a judge, and now in the dim light of the burning charcoal pots he rose to make judgment.

Was there to be no hearing for these poor people? What was the outlandish penalty for jaywalking? for shoving one's cart too close to the Enchanter's limousine? Was there to be no defense for these? no judge who would suspend sentence, say, "Not guilty!"? And where was the King?

The Enchanter lifted his hands. Small sparkles of light scattered from the movement. "My judgment," he said, "is that you are all guilty."

The people moaned and hung their heads in hopeless resignation.

"By rights you should be sentenced to burning, to forced labor, to the yielding of lands and possessions. But tonight—tonight is a night of celebration. The treasonous traitor has been captured. The one who has trafficked against my rules has been taken into my custody. In light of this, my pronouncement is that all sentences shall be reprieved. All the guilty in this courtroom shall be freed. There will only be one death tonight."

With this announcement the death drums quickened their rhythm, *Din-din din-din din-din din-din*. The prisoners stood in amazement. Such a thing had never happened in the history of Enchanted City. The guards unlocked wrist and leg bands; a woman reached toward the docket for her son. The clerk blew his trumpet as Breakers dispersed the amazed captives, who took to the benches and the back walls since all doors but one were barred and locked.

"Bring the miscreant forth!"

Amanda gasped. A man most unlike the King was dragged through the side door which led up from the dungeons. This was a disguise (if it was he) more than a disguise of apparel, or of wearing of common garments. It was a disguise of feature and form, of spirit and soul. The girl crept from her darkened corner and found a crowded space near an aisle in order to see.

Burners prodded him with their hot pokers; Breakers butted him with their cruel cudgels. Quietly, the man lifted his eyes and looked at the crowd in the courtroom. In that fleeting moment, Amanda recognized the look of her lord the King.

The names, she thought. *To His Majesty, my Soverign Leige . . .* she began, but the names, once so full of power, dropped in her thoughts like false coins,

tin, falling weightless on measuring scales. *The music*, she thought. But not one tune of Great Park could she remember. Though she had danced in the Great Celebration the night before, she couldn't recall one note.

She was powerless. What's more, the King was powerless.

Amanda wanted to scream, "Do something to save yourself! You are the King! The real King!"

The Enchanter leered, the yellow light in his eyes glowing. Amanda had seen that look before, that dragon play of the powerful sorcerer baiting a helpless victim before striking the deathblow.

The fire wizard leaned closer. "So," he said, and his voice was treacherous. "So, you are the true King and there is another Kingdom . . .?" He beat with his long fingers on the surface of the bench, raised an eyebrow, and smiled menacingly.

The man on trial answered not a word. He hung his head and refused to meet the Enchanter's gaze. This silence angered his accuser, who struggled to contain his growing wrath.

"So . . ." said the Enchanter, his voice rising. "So, you dare to challenge my dominion. You dare to raise insurrection and cause traffic jams in the streets. The chief of the Taxi Resistance is dead, but you—you! You are its reason. You are its inspiration. Death to pretenders!"

The courtroom grew warmer. Amanda felt as though her limbs were tied. Her heart throbbed painfully, beaten with the stick of terror. She felt faint and unbuttoned her warm vest. Then she realized she was unconsciously humming the song of the Naysayers. *"Nay-nay-nay; nay-nay-nay. Nothing can be done; nothing will be done; nothing is being done."* Oh, Mercie, she cried in her heart. *Oh, Caretaker. Help me! The King is ruined! We are all ruined!*

"First witness," cried the Clerk.

It was the Chief Herald, the one formerly known as Doublespeak. His friends said that he was Doublespeak no more, but Doomster, the one who pronounced judgment for the Enchanter. The emblem of the fire wizard was emblazoned on his elegant purple jersey; he wore brass armbands and a circlet of gold upon his head. "Why, I heard, I heard with my very own ears this man, this prisoner there, proclaim another kingdom, where the subjects live in the light. He attempted to entice me, me, the Chief Herald to the Enchanter, to treason."

Someone in the courtroom called out, "Treachery!" Another shouted, "Death to pretenders!"

The Clerk banged his gavel for order. The man in the center of the courtroom spoke not a word.

Amanda studied him carefully. His shoulders sagged as though he was suffering great sorrow. He seemed drawn within himself—the proceedings in that place made no difference. It was as though he had walked into a great aloneness and was not even present.

Seeing! thought Amanda. If she could see into the King's mind. Closing her eyes, Amanda aimed her gifts at the great soul of the man standing in disguise before her. A wave of enormous sadness overcame her. Tears began to stream down her cheeks and she was tempted to withdraw her sight. *"Nay-nay-nay,"* intoned the song of doom. The King's mind was entering into every dark place in Enchanted City—no, more—taking all the darkness into his very center.

Amanda could see nothing. The dark blindness overwhelmed her, but somehow she realized that her sight labored by the side of her dear King, the one she loved most in all the world.

"My Leige Lord," she whispered in her heart, and the man in front of her stirred slightly, as though he had heard and recognized her words with his own soul. It was then Amanda realized that nothing could be done, that for now, there was no light in the King, that he had for some reason of his own knowing joined with this deepest and most impenetrable darkness.

Through him Amanda stared into the shadow of death itself, into the night of all nights that begins and has no ending, and she withdrew, opening her eyes, unable to bear any more the grimacing features of total despair.

It was then she saw them, circling the rim of the courtyard, standing beyond and above and over the Burners and Breakers: gorgeous, brilliant, shining—the Bright Ones! They were translucent, shimmering. As Amanda glanced quickly at the miserable creatures sitting on benches, cold, shivering with fear, hopeless, glad for one wretched moment of reprieve at the expense of the most beautiful man who ever lived, the princess realized that no one else was aware of these creatures of indescribable glory.

Unknowing, they were all surrounded by these exquisite, unseen beings who glistened like raindrops on cobwebs blown by the wind, who turned like gossamer milkpod seeds in the brilliant sunlight, who raised their eyes filled with star glory, and stretched their wings, tip to tip, now gold, now silver, now pure light on light. The Bright Ones bent their graces toward the man in the center of this trial, preventing any interruption of purpose from breaking his intense concentration.

Their looks focused on the King in the center, holding off tenderness, staying any loving-kindness lest goodness distract him from the work of breaking the Enchanter's spell, which held all the city in its grip. They were not helping him; they were only keeping him from being interrupted. Amanda could see that they, too, wept.

The Princess turned her moist and opened eyes to the King. Now she understood that he was deliberately restraining his own power. He was not defeated by the gathering evil oppression in this hold of the fire wizard. The King was holding himself in, containing command and nobility, silencing his majestic authority, confining his royalty in order to descend by the way of mind and spirit into the center of dark agony, the very secret evil crux of the Enchanter's domain. He was preparing *himself* to be the willing victim who would lift the enchantment from the city.

It was then Amanda realized that the trial had gone on, that other witnesses had been called, that now the courtroom was a chaos of noise. "Burn him! Burn him!" the people screamed. "Death to the pretender!" pronounced the Chief Herald.

"TO THE BURNING PLACE!" screamed the Enchanter, and the iron cauldrons flared orange at the pronouncement of sentence. The death drums rolled. The pokers of the Burners glowed. The fire wizard removed his black robe of condemnation. The gavel pounded, raising sparks.

Amanda's heart broke at this judgment and she sobbed aloud, no longer hiding herself. For once it made no matter, for the evil eye sought only one victim, one sacrificial captive, and that One remained still, silent in the rising riot as the Enchanter began for procession of death.

So the Enchanter's men came a last time and took into custody the One who could walk into the center of madness, who could make his way into the underworld of each child's life, whose very name freed the prisoner, whose promise of a Kingdom made life worth playing, who brought light into all dark places. The One who could sing the whole song, who could call each orphan by name. The only One who could stare the Enchanter in the eye, who could challenge the very dominion of evil. The One who begins the dance of celebration again at life's end—the King, the true King.

The Burning Place

The Enchanter's time has come, the time for which he has so long waited. The power to end the influence of his hated challenger has fallen into his hand, the time when he will send his rival into final exile, into death itself.

"To the Burning Place!" shouts the Enchanter.

His cry pierces the night, and heralds quickly echo the sentence of doom. "Death!" they shout, "Death! Death!" as the drums beat in awful agreement, Oo-mb-pha . . . oo-mb-pha . . . oo-mb-pha-din. And the people standing in Traffic Court watch the proceedings and chant:

> "Burn him! Burn him!
> There is no such thing as a King!
> Death to Pretenders!
> The flames! The flames!"

Then the Burners close round the man. Their eyes beneath their dark hoods glow like gruesome embers set in coal; their pokers flash, red hot, now prodding, now poking, thrusting, wounding, searing brands without mercy.

"Death! Death!" cries the Chief Herald.

"Burn! Burn!" jeer the people.

"To the Burning Place!" screams the Enchanter again.

As the dreaded procession begins, each man, woman and child is drawn to the great mound of ashes on the edge of the City. Each vendor, each merchant, each worker within sound of the hearing of the drums responds to the call: oo-mb-pha, oo-mb-pha. As though by some dark magic, death captivates the citizens, beckoning them to the burning pyre to witness this drama of despair. Din-din, oo-mb-pha, oo-mb-pha, oo-mb-pha-din.

The Burners form an inner ring around the man, prodding him with hot irons. Breakers stand in an outer ring and push him with their cruel cudgels whenever he falters. Mercilessly they escort him from the central Dagoda, through the dark streets, past the heraldry posts, across the marketplace.

"Burn! Burn!" the crowd still cries. The children chase each other, skipping in time to the signal drums, chanting "Burning Place, Burning Place" as they run.

To Burning Place all come, where the ashes rise in choking clouds kicked up by the tromping mob. A pyre is readied in the center of the death field and a stake erected, thrusting solidly toward the deep night of the sky above Enchanted City.

A momentary silence, then the death drums roll anew. Fire priests circle the central pyre; the mob of Breakers approach. Rough hands lift the victim's battered body to the structure, the common cloth is torn from him, shoulder to ankle, his hands are bound behind the stake, his ankles tied, his head now sags. Fire priests prance the ceremonial steps; the bells sewn to the hem of their robes accent the rhythm of the death beats—jchang, jchang, jchang. Slowly, slowly, they step round and round the pyre, preparing for the sacrifice. Then silence, ominous silence as a single drum is beaten. Din. Din. Din.

In the hush, night presses on the heart, the lungs, the mind. The ashes of a thousand burnings scorch the nostrils of the people who push forward to see, to watch. And the subjects of the city understand at last: death touches all, breathes on each, whispers in every man's ear. All come to Burning Place, one sooner, one later, but all come.

Now the Enchanter's limousine, long, sleek, black, silent, draws to the edge of Burning Place. The Enchanter emerges, his eyes hot with anticipation, his robe an image of woven flame. All clear a wide path for him; none wish to touch him in his heat or feel his burning gaze.

But he has eyes only for One, for the mauled figure tied to the stake, standing bound on the pyre above the crowd. The fire wizard lifts his hands, throws back his head, and begins to dance in triumphant celebration. He is an ogre of glee, chortling, shooting flames, flashing now light, now dark, calling the night unto himself until the people of Enchanted City gasp for air. They choke, and the head of the sacrificial one droops lower.

The Enchanter dances one complete circuit around the pyre, then stops and bows in mockery. The Burners hold their glowing pokers at salute, the death drums roll in unison again, the ghastly Breakers raise their cudgels.

Death to Pretenders—the spoken words are soft. All lean forward to hear. The fire priests swing from the pyre to the ashes below, except for one who waits to light the stacked wood.

"Death to Pretenders."

A wind starts to blow, raising ash dust.

"DEATH TO PRETENDERS!"

A torch is lit. The priest touches it to the pyre. The flames burst into the night. They whoosh; they burn; they leap higher and higher. The wild wind roars, feeding the conflagration. The shadow at the stake lifts, arches, raises its head, and is crowned with burning.

The Enchanter is a writhing, frenzied sillouhette before the fire. He lifts his distorted face to the flames, "Owa-ha-ha! Owa-ha-ha!"—the howl of a beast over its prey. OWA-HA-HA! OWA-HA-HA!

But each common man stands pierced to the soul, watching the crackling flames, the leaping cinders, the chorus of fire singing raucously upon the pyre. For all know now, though they may forget it tomorrow: the wizard will feel joy at any burning place, at any death time, at any agony of final passing. He will preside in gleeful dance at any dying.

At this moment, out of the flame, some say out of the shadow in the middle of the flame, an intense light blazes, more than fire, more than burning. It explodes out over them, cracking the gathering darkness, splitting it momentarily before its dawn time, bursting with such ferocity that all shield their eyes and hide their faces and turn their backs from the center.

Just as suddenly it is night again, blackest of blackest night. In despair, the people begin to leave, feeling their way in the terrible darkness back to their hovels, to the hidden hideaways of this city of unspeakable doom. Death has done what it always will do.

A young woman stands disbelieving at the edge of the ashes. Once madness captured her in its carnival circle, tossing her round and round in its ceaseless unhappy endings. Then a man came into the center of her torture and looked into her eyes, bringing sanity and giving her a reason to look deeply into the eyes of any man or woman. And what is left for her? Madness again?

Two young men, friends, support each other and stand at a distance before the pyre. They strangle on their tears. Into the cold depths of their underworld a man had come and led them into the warmth of light and fire and had taught them to sing the joyous whole melody of the partial tune they had once only feebly hummed. Will there ever be music again? Will the musicians tune their instruments and the orchestra play? Will the dancers step the steps once more, and laugh as they dance? Or will the song never again be sung?

A beautiful woman with flaxen hair falls to her knees in the ash dust. Will she never again act out stories in the streets? Will the tales of love and courage be forgotten? Will she nevermore speak the rhymes of peace, the poetry of hope, the prose of power? Will the memory of the tale be broken, the most wonderful story of all be locked away in the archives, never to be retold?

Two boys pray together, but no words come. Will language again be crooked, halting, tongue-tied? Will the words all be twisted, stammered, and backwards? Will mouths swell and spew forth wickedness? Will goodness never again find speech?

In the darkness, a crowd begins to gather, a throng—all those who have loved and served the King, all those who have worked in the resistance; each man, woman, and child who ever dared to believe in the breaking of enchantments or dared to hope in a future restoration. All who longed for the exile to end now stand mourning in the ashes of the death of all dreams and try to remember light, and song, and life.

The Keeper of the Chronicle of Sightings of the King stands silent, too, stripped of hope, ravaged. The Enchanter is the victor after all, death his second-in-command. *There is no such thing as a Kingdom*, he thinks. *Great Park is only make-believe. Mercie, Caretaker, Ranger Commander—we are all just pretenders. I am no Hero, nor a King's man. The city saying is so: "There is no such thing as a King." This is and will ever be the keep of the Great Enchanter.*

He holds the handle of the hatchet by his side, feeling no power. *We have tricked ourselves*, he thinks and casts the tool to the ground. Then he sits in the ashes, his heart too much of stone for weeping.

He stares at the gathering crowd, shadows in the blackness. *Why are they here? It's all over. We all are orphans, all ugly deformed scarboys, sewer rats and boiler brats, carnival girls, heralds of untruths.* And we must all return to Enchanted City, this place of the no-people. The time for heroics is ended.

He sits motionless; he sleeps but sees no visions. Numb, he rests not. He wakes to darkness; no day comes. Will this night never end? All is done. Over. Never to be again, a forever unhappiness.

In the night, he thinks that the shadows, forms deeper than the substance of darkness, creep closer to the pyre which rises black, a rubble of twisted cinder and charcoal, in the middle of Burning Place. Someone stands beside him, and reaches to him a hand. It is an old, old woman, more bent than ever, the grasp now feeble. It is Mercie.

"Why are they here?" he asks her, motioning to the shadows. "Must all who love him come?"

Her voice is weak; her answer sounds far away. "Yes. All who love the King must come to this place before they can see the Restoration begin."

He wants to scoff. He wants to shout silence, but his eye is caught by a tiny glow on the pyre—*embers that are not completely burned.* Others in the gathered congregation of shadows see it, too; they gasp. Peering, he rises to his knees, but wait! The glow suddenly becomes a flame, one small warm ring of light, not an angry destroying rage, but a good burning, a flower flame, growing strangely larger and larger, unfolding upon itself, petals of soft fire, layer upon layer opening outward, white, rose, golden, glowing.

In this sudden light, he can see that the shadows are the people of Great Park who have stood in the darkness, waiting, waiting. Here a band of Rangers in forest garb. There orphans newly arrived, their faces scrubbed but filled with anxiety. He spies Amanda. This has been a night of anguish for her; her face is haggard, but her eyes—they seem to be filled with sight. And beyond them all, strange forms of soft, almost indistinguishable luminescence.

As the flower of fire grows, he sees his comrades from the taxi resistance, people of the city, brave men and women whose faces are now filling with wonder. Nearby stands Caretaker, his back straightening in the warmth of the new flame.

Then out of the center of the lovely burning light, a laugh! His heart leaps. He has heard that laugh before. His being lurches with hope.

It is the laugh of the King!

All stare into the middle of the death field, into the flaming flower, their mouths agape, their eyes open wide. A form is taking shape in the middle of the pistils and the stamen. A real form is rising from the burning center. It gathers unto itself, becoming distinct, definite, firm. The watchers narrow their vision in order to see better what they can scarcely believe they are seeing. It's the King—the King! He stands tall, stands bold. He stamps a foot—sending flames dancing into the night. He lifts his arms in exultation.

He throws back his head and laughs—the challenger, the conqueror laughs the first laugh of creation again and again and again.

Suddenly, in the middle of that blackest night, right at midnight, when stars, moons, and planets are utterly dimmed by enchantment, day comes. Light splits the darkness again. Day falls upon Enchanted City—shafts of glorious light, brilliant rays of brightness, dawning come untimely. And the King in the center of the burning field lifts his face to the warm new sun and at that, the flowering fire quiets and the King steps from the flames.

And all see at once that he is the meaning of the dance; he is the other side of the death place, his word weaves universe out of chaos; he is the restorer of all lost cities; his life is the potion all must take against enchantment.

The great crowd of subjects of the King ring Burning Place. A circle, a great vast circle, stretches around the dusty rim of the death field. They join hands, reaching to their neighbor, young to old, woman to man, adult to child. From the center of the burning flower, quieted but still luxuriant with light, the familiar music begins. It is the music of the Great Celebration. *Ah-h-h-h-h,* they have heard this before; *ah-h-h-h-h,* slowly, very slowly, the great circle begins to turn.

Hero watches the graceful movements. But the people are not changed. Is becoming over? *Will we never be real again,* he wonders, *become who we really are?*

"Hero!" a Ranger friend calls. "Are you no longer dancing?"

The music quickens as the King in the center stoops and lifts an armful of flame which shimmers and flutters in his embrace, alive. And as the dance passes, he tosses a flower to this one, to that until the whole moving ring is filled with brilliant light, like comets, like galaxies of orbiting moons. And Hero watches as each now becomes, not passing through the Circle of Sacred Flames, but being passed through themselves by holy light as the shining fires disappear only to shine brightly from each one's eyes.

Then the King, the King himself, cries to Hero, "Keeper of the Chronicle! Light?" And when he turns his face, it is then that Hero sees the mark. A scar new from the burning, a scar like his own—but not like it. It is not the Enchanter's mark, not stamped into the flesh by hot iron. It is like a flower high on the cheekbone, like a crown, like a red and perfect rose. Lifting his hand to his face, Hero discovers that the rough fleshly rim of his own scar has disappeared. The mark of branding has been forever healed.

Overwhelmed, all Hero can do is laugh—the Enchantment truly is broken! And his feet, almost despite themselves, begin to step to the music, and he draws himself up proud, standing tall, a subject of the King, this most beautiful of men *alive*. And he is proud to be called a King's man.

"LIGHT!" he calls back.

The King tosses the dancing fire his way, and Hero's head is bathed in warmth as he feels the wonderful homespun wool of the cloak of Ranger blue falling around his shoulders, and he is lighted through and through. He breathes the sudden cool air of Great Park, fragrant with field and flower. He looks into the eye of street urchin and orphan, and they are truly beautiful. And his soul feels bold; at heart he knows he is a man of courage.

Nearby, Mercie's luxuriant black hair falls to her waist; she is once again the most beautiful of women. Ranger Commander, strong, broad shouldered and grand, bows to his warrior wife. Amanda, in her royal garments, dances in the ring way across the field. Hero watches as the circle moves closer, and he sees the old gladsome laughter in her eyes. He meets her to take her hand and to join the dance beside her as they all, subjects of the Kingdom, laugh and sing and step the sacred steps round and round this Most Royal Highness, His Majesty the King.

It is only then, when the circle is finally fulfilled, and each one he loves has become real with sacred starshine in their eyes, that the King himself turns in motion to the sweet, solemn and glorious music of Great Park. Then, while his own eyes shine with day, he lifts his hands to the light, and in this first morning of the beginning again of all time, he proclaims aloud, "The Enchantment is broken! **LET THE RESTORATION BEGIN!"**